# MARCO POLO

# DEVON & CORNWALL

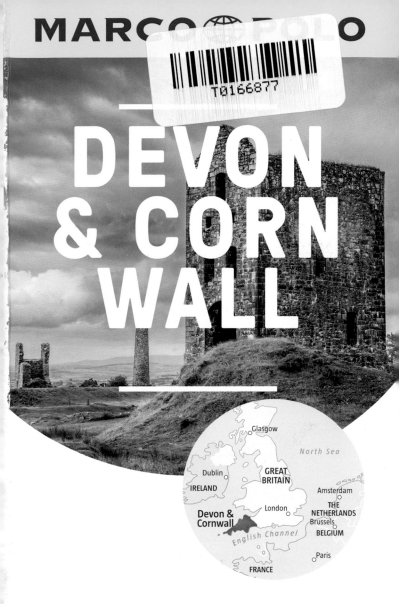

Glasgow

*North Sea*

Dublin

**GREAT BRITAIN**

**IRELAND**

Amsterdam

**THE NETHERLANDS**

London

Devon & Cornwall

Brussels

**BELGIUM**

*English Channel*

Paris

**FRANCE**

# THE TOURING APP

shows you the way...
including routes and offline maps!

FREE!

# GET MORE OUT OF YOUR MARCO POLO GUIDE

## IT'S AS SIMPLE AS THIS

**1** go.marco-polo.com/dco

**2** download and discover

# GO!

WORKS OFFLINE!

---

**SYMBOLS**

 Insider Tip

★ Highlight

●●●● Best of ...

☼ Scenic view

♺ Responsible travel: fair
trade principles and the
environment respected

(*) Telephone numbers
that are not toll-free

**PRICE CATEGORIES HOTELS**

| | |
|---|---|
| *Expensive* | over £105 |
| *Moderate* | £60–105 |
| *Budget* | under £60 |

The prices are for two people
sharing per night, including
breakfast

**PRICE CATEGORIES RESTAURANTS**

| | |
|---|---|
| *Expensive* | over £17 |
| *Moderate* | £9–17 |
| *Budget* | under £9 |

The prices are for a standard
meal for each restaurant
without drinks

# CONTENTS

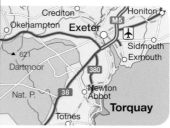

---

**DID YOU KNOW?**
Timeline → p. 14
Local specialities → p. 28
Explore Cornwall's mines
→ p. 43
For bookworms and film buffs
→ p. 59
On the trail of the dinosaurs
→ p. 71
On the smugglers' route → p. 83
Public holidays → p. 107
Budgeting → p. 111
Currency converter → p. 113
Weather → p. 114

**MAPS IN THE GUIDEBOOK**
(118 A1) Page numbers
and coordinates refer
to the road atlas
(0) Site/address located off
the map.
Coordinates are also given for
places that are not marked
on the road atlas
(U A1) refers to the
city maps for Exeter and
Plymouth on the back
cover

(🛇 A–B 2–3) refers to
the removable pull-out map
(🛇 a–b 2–3) refers to the
additional inset map on the
pull-out map

**INSIDE FRONT COVER:**
The best Highlights

**INSIDE BACK COVER:**
City maps for Exeter and
Plymouth

# The best MARCO POLO Insider Tips

## Our top 15 Insider Tips

**INSIDER TIP** **Dreaming in the lighthouse**

The St Anthony Lighthouse near St Mawes not only looks amazing: you can also stopover here in a *holiday flat* → **p. 35**

**INSIDER TIP** **Ice cream made from creamy organic milk**

Happy cows produce tasty milk, *Roskilly's* near St Keverne makes delicious ice cream with it (photo right) → **p. 39**

**INSIDER TIP** **Reasonable and with a sea view**

Who says that budget hotels must always be bad? The *Travelodge* in Newquay has plenty of rooms with fabulous sea views → **p. 40**

**INSIDER TIP** **Lights on!**

When the Advent candles are lit, the village of Mousehole switches on its *Christmas Lights*. They illuminate the harbour throughout the festive season until the start of January → **p. 107**

**INSIDER TIP** **By train along the coast**

If you set off on the *Looe Valley Line* to the fishing port of Looe, you can admire the picturesque scenery along the route → **p. 55**

**INSIDER TIP** **Overnight accommodation with the star chef**

TV chef Rick Stein is famous for his exclusive restaurants – in Padstow, he now owns his own boutique *St Petroc's Hotel* → **p. 56**

**INSIDER TIP** **May Day celebrations**

May festivals are not just for trade unionists. In Cornwall, the entire town of Padstow celebrates the *Obby Oss Festival* on 1 May – with plenty of dancing, music and exceptional food (photo top) → **p. 56**

**INSIDER TIP** **Coffee from the moor**

The nation of tea drinkers has discovered the taste: *DJ Miles* has a roastery for fine coffees in the village of Porlock on Exmoor → **p. 80**

**INSIDER TIP** A day of quiet contemplation

Lambs, puffins and water everywhere – *Lundy Island* is a place for explorers and those who like peace and quiet. If you want to get closer to the little island, you can easily do so during the summer months and take a day trip by boat → **p. 85**

**INSIDER TIP** Relaxing on the Atlantic

*Hartland Quay Hotel* may not be a luxury hotel, but it offers a breathtaking view of the Hartland coast as well as a small history museum → **p. 83**

**INSIDER TIP** Fantastic route for cyclists

*The Granite Way* is a fantastic way of exploring the foothills of legendary Dartmoor by bicycle. The route heads along a disused rail track from Okehampton to Meldon Viaduct → **p. 63**

**INSIDER TIP** Enjoy a pint in the open-air

Why stay sitting inside the pub? *The Imperial* in Exeter has a lovely and spacious beer garden in summer → **p. 67**

**INSIDER TIP** Good quality local products

Products from the local region are popular in Devon and Cornwall – the best example is the *Farm Store* at Powderham Castle → **p. 68**

**INSIDER TIP** Potent plants

*Torre Abbey* is not only a historic building in Torquay: plants grow in its garden that were used as poisonous concoctions in Agatha Christie's novels → **p. 74**

**INSIDER TIP** Teatime in style

The *Imperial Hotel* in Torquay continues the pleasant British tradition of *afternoon tea.* Enjoy teatime and the fabulous surrounding views → **p. 75**

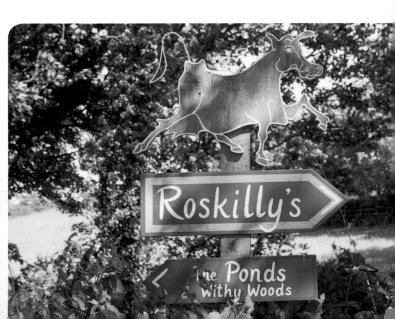

# BEST OF ...

**FOR FREE**

● *Castles for free*

Visiting historic sights such as castles and palaces can be pricey. But once a year the owners of several thousand British attractions open for free – on the *Heritage Open Days,* always at the start of September → p. 52

● *Free admission in museums*

Many museums now also charge admission, but not the *Sidmouth Museum* in this Devon town: here, you can find out about the *Jurassic Coast* and its fossils → p. 71

● *Taste cider*

Cider is delicious! *Healeys Cornish Cyder Farm* not only makes cider, but also opens its production facilities to visitors for free. Free samples are also available, you only need to pay for a guided tour → p. 36

● *Exeter guided tour for free*

City tours can be expensive – that's why Exeter (photo) started the *Red Coat Guided Tours*: city walks that everybody can join for free. There are at least two walks daily, starting from the cathedral → p. 66

● *Play tennis free of charge*

Tennis usually involves high club or court fees. The campaign *Tennis for Free* aims to change this across the country: in Exeter and Plymouth free coaching sessions are available, the only requirement is to book ahead → p. 101

● *Church services in cathedrals*

England's old cathedrals like *Exeter Cathedral* are impressive architectural monuments. Many churches charge admission to help with the maintenance costs. If you attend a church service on Sundays, you can go inside for free → p. 64

○○○● Dots in guidebook refer to "Best of" tips

# ONLY IN DEVON & CORNWALL
## Unique experiences

● *Cream tea with scones*
No trip to Devon or Cornwall is complete without a genuine *cream tea*. But what goes on the *scone* first — is it cream or jam? Start your research at the *Chapel Cafe* at Port Isaac Pottery near Padstow → **p. 57**

● *Hiking along the coast*
The white acorn on a brown background shows the way: the *South West Coast Path* circles the whole of Devon and Cornwall. It's a great opportunity to explore both counties in hiking gear. You don't need to finish the entire route and can walk along a short section → **p. 83**

● *A pint in the pub*
What would Britain be without pubs? Meet for a pint in the local pub and take the opportunity to chat to the locals. For example in the Lanivet Inn in Bodmin → **p. 50**

● *Where England begins*
An island always has several farthest landmarks and *Land's End* is one of them in Great Britain: the westernmost point of England is where the kingdom begins → **p. 42**

● *Gardens galore*
Landscape gardens are almost compulsory for any large country estate in Devon and Cornwall — after all, plenty of plants grow here that don't flourish elsewhere in Great Britain. An exceptionally lovely example are the *Lost Gardens of Heligan* (photo) → **p. 44**

● *Places for water sports fans*
Water sports are a way of life in Devon and Cornwall. The coastline offers numerous beaches for bathing, surfing and diving — particularly popular spots are *Newquay* in Cornwall and *Exmouth* in Devon → **p. 40, p. 69**

ONLY IN

# BEST OF ...

● **The earth's climatic zones**
The *Eden Project* (photo) recreates the earth's climatic zones under huge biomes, which are reliable without rain, even if they tend to have high humidity. Where else in England can you experience temperatures of 30° C/80 °F and more in winter? → p. 44

● **Watch the fishes at eye level**
It's better to look at the aquarium from indoors than getting wet outdoors: the *National Marine Aquarium* in Plymouth not only displays fishes from all over the world, but also has the deepest tank in the country → p. 71

● **Visit the caves**
In *Kents Cavern,* the oldest system of caves in Great Britain, nobody minds the weather – the temperatures are constant here where humans already lived hundreds of thousands of years ago → p. 74

● **Jump into warm water**
At the *Waterworld* leisure pool in Newquay you can spend the entire day and forget about the rain. It's also fabulous for children! → p. 103

● **Art from London**
Who says that you have to travel to London to see wonderful artworks? Tate Gallery, one of the country's top museums, has opened a branch in Cornwall! In *Tate St Ives*, masterpieces are on display – indoors and dry! – from the gallery's collection → p. 45

● **Shop and save**
Why spend lots of money shopping when you can find bargains? The *Atlantic Village* outlet shopping centre near Bideford offers designer products at discounted prices. You'll soon forget the bad weather! → p. 80

**RAIN**

# RELAX AND CHILL OUT
## Take it easy and spoil yourself

● *Revive in the spa*
Re-energise and do something good for your mind and body – that's easy in one of the spas in Cornwall. For example, the *Watergate Bay Hotel* in Newquay offers fabulous spa packages → **p. 40**

● *Close your eyes on the beach*
Relax on one of the numerous beaches – close your eyes and listen to the waves and feel the soft sand, for instance, on *Burgh Island* in Devon → **p. 73**

● *Relax on a seaward trip*
A *day trip to the Isles of Scilly* is not only an adventure because of the destination – during the boat crossing you can enjoy the open sea. Lean back and breathe in the sea air, while you look forward to exploring a unique corner of England → **p. 35**

● *Train with a view*
Great Britain offers several of the most beautiful train routes in Europe. One of these is in South Devon between Paignton and King-swear. It's so relaxing to take a seat in one of the old carriages of the *Dartmouth Steam Railway* and enjoy the views through the window of the coast, sea and forest while you travel → **p. 65**

● *Open-air pool with a sea view*
Lidos have a long tradition in England. One of the most famous lidos has recently been renovated: at the *Jubilee Pool* in Penzance you can swim, chillax on the sun loungers or simply admire the amazing sea view (photo) → **p. 42**

● *Heavenly choirs*
England's choirs are world famous – it's hardly surprising that almost every church offers beautiful music. That includes the cathedral in Truro where you can enjoy listening to the *Choral Evensong* on weekdays from 5.30pm → **p. 46**

INTRODUCTION

# DISCOVER DEVON AND CORNWALL!

Lush green meadows, dramatic rocky cliffs between quaint villages, beautiful country houses and the occasional old-fashioned red telephone box. If you think of *quintessential England*, you usually picture the landscapes of Devon and Cornwall. Both the *south-western counties* perfectly reflect the natural beauty of the British countryside. They offer abundant architectural treasures. The people are also unique in this part of the British Isles which were once part of an empire. Despite the rumours, the weather is often pleasant. Thanks to the effect of the Gulf Stream, the temperatures rarely fall below zero. Summers are warm but not too hot. Palm trees even grow in the front gardens.

Some areas of Cornwall are even known as the *English Riviera* because of the especially mild temperatures here. Devon and Cornwall therefore count among the most popular holiday regions in the United Kingdom.

Devon & Cornwall's rich literary history has lured many travellers. You can discover *picture book scenes* around almost every bend. Against the backdrop of grand country estates, bleak moorland and exquisite harbours, it is fascinating to imagine Poldark returning to Cornwall from America or Hercule Poirot,

Ponies grazing on an isolated part of Dartmoor

Agatha Christie's famous detective, uncovering a gruesome murder in this beautiful picturesque landscape.

Newquay in south-west Cornwall has long since emerged as one of *Europe's top surfing spots*. Surfer dudes from all over the world are enticed here during the summer to champion the waves on their boards. In the evening, they relax

and party in the pub or on the beach where – another cliché – they like to park the occasional VW camper van. Devon's capital city Exeter is a university city with an *excellent reputation for research*. International scholars are attracted here from many different countries. While the idyllic old town around the *majestic cathedral* is regarded as one of England's top attractions, a lively student scene has developed and, of course, suitably *buzzing nightlife.* In the early evening, the many pubs make ideal meeting places. Sooner or later, in the big cities the nightclub becomes a focal point and the sound of loud music spills onto the street.

> **Trinket shops and top surf spots for surfer dudes**

Life in the countryside is much quieter. In central Devon, on Exmoor, Dartmoor and along the Cornish coast *time has apparently stood still*. While the major fashion chains fill the high streets elsewhere, here the local retailers have held their ground. There are *numerous small shops* offering all kinds of trinkets along with fishing rods or a pint of milk. The locals call these shops quirky. It's invariably true and intended as a compliment. Most visitors are attracted here precisely because things are *quirky*.

the Angels and Saxons form the basis of the legends of King Arthur

**1066**
William the Conqueror defeats King Harold II near Hastings. A new era begins for the island

**1215**
Magna Carta is signed. To the present day, this is the foundation of British law

**1534**
Henry VIII establishes the Anglican church and breaks away from Rome

**1588**
Sir Francis Drake defeats the Spanish Armada from Devon

Many residents in this region of Britain are friendly. Visitors are generally welcomed everywhere and the hospitality is exceptional. At the same time, many people who were born here are patriotic about their county.

In Cornwall, you often see a black flag with a white cross – this is the county flag. The Cornish standard flies outside homes and is displayed in the rear windows of cars. *Cornish*, which has almost died out as a Celtic language, is currently being taught again. The county's location in a remote south-westerly part of Great Britain often *feels like an insular island*. London is four to five hours away. Many locals are only moderately interested in the decision-making process in the British capital.

> ## It's not surprising that fresh fish is on the menu here

For the locals in *small fishing villages*, the day's catch is often more important than new legislation passed by the British parliament. Despite the increased competition, fishing trawlers from several Cornish ports – Newlyn, Coverack, Brixton – still set out to catch sardines, cod and other fish. It's not surprising that fresh fish is on the menu in almost every restaurant. The tiny coastal villages, where nobody puts to sea any longer, still show signs of their fishing heritage. Small restaurants, pubs and souvenir shops have opened in the *old harbours*.

Devon and Cornwall became popular tourist destinations in the 19th century. Those who live in the south-west have long taken pride in the fact that visitors love to travel here. This explains why you can still find so many cosy and traditional hotels and restaurants. However, the region has attracted considerable investment with large hotel chains setting up new establishments with a different luxurious style. Most smaller hoteliers have embraced the change. They now offer *relaxing and luxury getaways*. Many are now classed as boutique hotels, while others offer spa packages.

Although there are no royal palaces in this part of the country, other aristocratic families still maintain *country house estates*, such as Pendennis Castle

**1620**
The "Mayflower" sets out from Plymouth with the first English settlers departing for America

**1833**
The building of the Great Western Railway marks the steady pace of industrialisation in Devon and Cornwall. Tourism gains in importance

**1952**
Elizabeth II becomes Queen

**1998**
South Crofty Mine closes, ending 4,000 years of mining in Cornwall

**2016**
In a referendum, Britons vote by a narrow majority for their country to leave the EU

A romantic setting: fishing boats along the coast of the Lizard Peninsula

**Country houses in unique settings**

in Falmouth, St Mawes Castle and St Michael's Mount Castle. Many of the buildings are in a unique setting – on steep rocky outcrops, in undulating grasslands or by isolated river estuaries. Holidaymakers are mainly attracted to explore the natural environment. This is an ideal location for *hiking tours*. It is well worth walking along the South West Coast Path, which extends 1,000 km/621 mi along the coastline. Cycling routes are becoming increasingly popular: the countrywide National Cycle Network has converted a magnificent network of paths and disused rail tracks to *traffic free cycle routes*.

Two *unique landmarks* are also situated in Cornwall: England's southernmost Lizard Point and the westernmost landmark at Land's End. Both lie in fabulous coastal areas, although unfortunately they are also overrun with tourists. It's best to leave the crowds behind to explore the coastal path. Alternatively, you can get away on a boat and explore *one of the most beautiful island groups* in Great Britain: the Isles of Scilly. The islands are situated at the westernmost point of England about 45 km/28 mi off Land's End. But why hurry to arrive at the end of such a beautiful part of the world? The attraction of Devon and Cornwall is much greater. After all, there is still so much to explore!

# WHAT'S HOT

## 1 Inner Ariel

*Mermaid Diving* Glide through the water like Ariel, the mermaid! *Mermaid Diving* is the name for a new sports craze in Cornwall where women and men put on a mermaid tail fin and learn to dive like a fish. Since the Newquay-based diving school *Freedive UK (tel. 01637 62 19 22 | www.freediveuk.com)* first offered the course, the hype has been non-stop. Everyone wants to learn to be a mermaid! Courses are available for one, three or four days – but hurry because places soon get fully booked.

## Group picnic 2

*Outdoor feasts together* *Feast Nights* are a new style of group event that's ultimately about one thing: food. Everybody packs plates, wine and cutlery and meets at organised venues to be fed. Everything is in the open-air and the atmosphere is relaxed. But one thing gets special attention: the quality of the food. *Feast Nights* are genuine festivals for foodies. Venues which offer these events include *Nancarrow Farm (Zelah | tel. 01872 54 03 43 | www.nancarrowfarm.co.uk/events/feast-nights)* and the *Hidden Hut (Porthcurnick Beach | Portscatho | www.hiddenhut.co.uk/feast-nights)*.

## 3 Favourite drink

*Gin renaissance* Although the gin craze was never quite over, England is enjoying a gin revival. There are numerous innovative and flavoursome spirits. Pubs also offer a wide selection of craft gins. *Dolly's Bar (21 Church Street | tel. 01326 21 84 00 | www.dollysbar.co.uk)* in Falmouth has more than 130 gin varieties. The *Southwestern Distillery (www.southwesterndistillery.com)* in St Ervan produces *Tarquin's*, a gin which is locally made in Cornwall.

There are lots of new things to discover in Devon and Cornwall. A few of the most interesting are listed below

# Luxury tents

*Glamping*  At first, it was dismissed as a passing trend, but now it has quickly caught on in this part of the country. New camping sites have sprung up in many places with chic, spacious tents with every imaginable luxury – some are even small huts with a jacuzzi or shower. Popular glamping sites are *Trecombe Lakes (www.trecombe-lakes.co.uk)* near Falmouth and *Ready Camp (www.campingandcaravanningclub.co.uk)* near Tavistock. But before making a reservation, please note that one night in a luxury pad is almost as expensive as a hotel.

# Design classics

*Oldtimers*  Touring across England like James Bond in a 1960s film. Although cars are becoming sportier, the British have re-discovered their love of the classic models. MGs, the timeless Mini, Jaguar – genuine car enthusiasts appreciate the vintage designs. Car hire companies now specialise in oldtimers. It's not exactly cheap (you can expect to pay £100 to £150 per day), but it's great fun! A specialist company in Devon is *Self Drive Classics (Wrangaton | tel. 079 18 71 50 39 | www.selfdriveclassics.co.uk).* You can hire the surfers' favourite, a classic Volkswagen camper van from *O'Connors (Old Road | Okehampton | tel. 01837 65 95 99 | www.oconnorscampers.co.uk)* and *Cornish Campers (Higher Trevesson Barn | Gorran | tel. 01726/84 28 00 | www.cornishcampers.co.uk).*

# IN A NUTSHELL

## THIS WEATHER IS FICKLE

It's not all mists, constant rain and biting cold! In Devon and Cornwall, palms seem to grow in every front garden. These plants originate from South America and the Canary Islands. Although rather unusual in England, palm trees are common in these counties with the milder climate. The Gulf Stream flows past the south coast of Great Britain. It rarely snows in this region, and the temperatures in winter almost never fall below zero.

Rain showers are frequent, but this is also why the lawns are so green. Constant rain is rare here. Short sharp showers are more usual and they are often unexpected. The island location can also mean that while flooding affects the roads on Dartmoor, only a few miles away in Exeter the sun is shining. British people love talking about the weather. The morning weather forecast is an essential part of the day!

## ENGLAND'S SURFERS' PARADISE

Forget castles and sheep – Devon and Cornwall are both a lot hipper than you might think. In the summer, young people from all over the world transform parts into something that looks like the British Surfers' Paradise. You can find old Volkswagen vans at the beaches, during the day well-tanned hipsters throw themselves into the waves, in the evening they celebrate life in trendy

**From tea to trendy fashions:
Devon and Cornwall delight in traditions
but always embrace what's new**

bars. Fistral Beach and Watergate Bay are Newquay's two main beaches for surfing. Throughout the town you will find backpacker accommodation and Australian style pubs. Surfing here is not just a sport – it is a way of life. Newquay has become so hip that some have long since moved on to the beaches along the coast at Ilfracombe which are more than a good substitute. Woolacombe is ideal for families and beginners, whilst Croyde Bay is for experts. In the 1920s the sport spread from the Pacific region to the Channel Islands before surfers also discovered the ideal conditions off the Cornish coast. Today, surfing is a kind of antidote to the tranquil image of the area.

# THE MURDERER IS ...

How can anyone ever get the idea of committing a murder in this lovely landscape? Agatha Christie, with some two billion books sold, is the world's most successful criminologist and committed quite a few in Devon and

Market fresh: fish and seafood aplenty

Cornwall — at least in her books. The writer, born in Torquay, spent a few years here in the south-west, and later in life, spent many months at her Greenway Estate near Dartmouth which can be found in her novel *"Dead Man's Folly"*, amongst others. Christie was quite attached to the Burgh Island Hotel on Devon's south coast, which is why she used it as the crime scene for "Evil Under the Sun". The author published 66 crime novels, with Miss Marple and Hercule Poirot she invented two of the most famous detectives in literary history. Another, Sherlock Holmes, is not created by her, but by Sir Arthur Conan Doyle — and he also went to Devon for investigations. "The Hound of Baskerville" is set on Dartmoor and the author researched the site long and hard. John le Carré, on the other hand, moved a little farther west: for over forty years, the master of the spy empire lived in St. Buryan in Cornwall and loved it so much that he even acquired about a mile of coastline.

# THE LAND OF GARDENS AND PARKS

His reputation is like the Shakespeare of garden design — in the 18th century, Lancelot "Capability" Brown invented classical English garden design which is still world famous. Brown designed about 170 estates in Great Britain, which highlights the importance of garden splendour in England. No manor house or castle grounds lack an artfully designed parkland. Several dozen designers later imitated Brown's landscape gardens.

Devon and Cornwall also offers numerous beautiful parks and gardens. There is little inclination to change this. In the south-west, traditions are especially appreciated and carefully cultivated.

## ROUND AND ROUND

The roads in Devon and Cornwall can put drivers in a spin, as they are full of roundabouts. Apparently, virtually all the villages, country roads or motorway slip roads lead into a roundabout.

## REGIONAL STYLE

Country house fashion with a Barbour jacket and herringbone sports jacket? That's outdated! In Devon and Cornwall popular fashion labels have developed and fashion items now fill the wardrobes of school pupils and students up and down the country. *Jack Wills* from Salcombe in Devon offers understated, high-quality college fashion to rival trendy American labels like Abercrombie & Fitch and Gap. *Saltrock*, founded in Penzance, is a surfer label with similar sportswear to the popular brands Quiksilver or Element. *Seasalt* originates from Falmouth in Cornwall and produces modern, summery women's fashion collections. These fashion labels have retail stores in every larger town in south-west England.

## FISH IS ON THE MENU

An island without fish is almost unthinkable. Fishing is still a way of life on the southern English coast. British fishermen bring in about 600,000 tonnes of fish every year. This is significantly less than major competitors in Asia and overseas, but enough to supply the island's restaurants and markets with the best quality fish. The EU catch quotas set tight controls for fishermen in the United Kingdom. In Devon and Cornwall's small fishing ports, many locals already hope for a positive change of this situation due to Brexit. They expect that they might be allowed unrestricted fishing rights in the English Channel. Accordingly, alarm bells are ringing for environmental campaigners. Currently, great-tasting fresh fish and seafood from the British Isles is unrivalled. This applies not only to the ever-popular *fish & chips*. You should also sample more exotic seafood like scallops or oysters which are frequently on the menu and at reasonable prices.

## NEXT STOP: CORNWALL

In a nationwide survey in 2002 the BBC made him the second greatest Briton after Winston Churchill: Isambard Kingdom Brunel is not just any engineer – he is the master of Victorian Britain. One of his masterpieces is the Great Western Railway, which since 1841 first linked London to Bristol and was latterly extended to Plymouth and Penzance. The six-hour journey between Paddington and Cornwall is still one of the most charming railway routes in England. It leads through the Thames Valley and along the coast of Devon – which is why GWR, the abbreviation of the railway company, was formerly translated as "God's Wonderful Railway". Even today a night train runs between London and Penzance as well as many more trains during the day.

# SPEAK KERNOWEK

Cornish heritage, from a linguistic point of view, has really suffered. In 1891, the last person who spoke Cornish fluently, in everyday life, died. Since then, the dialect of the Celts, which is akin to Welsh and Breton, has been under threat of dying out. It's had a long history. After the Romans withdrew in 407, the Anglo-Saxons pushed the Celtic population westwards to Wales and Cornwall. In the eastern part of Cornwall, educated people very quickly took up the English language, while in the western parts most of the families spoke only Kernowek until the 17th century. Today, it is officially recognised as a minority language by the UK government and is even re-taught. Today's modern Cornish is a reconstruction of the extinct language with the help of traditions and written testimonies. Radio stations transmit single programmes in the old dialect and in 2011 even the Bible was published in Cornish.

# HISTORY SET IN STONE

Everybody has heard of Stonehenge. Did you know that stone circles also exist in Devon and Cornwall? Experts assume that natural resources such as tin and copper attracted people here during the Neolithic period. Apparently, our early ancestors loved to transport the stones from one end of the island to the other, creating fascinating stone circles or stacking them to build a stone hut. Why? The subject leads to repeated controversy, but the experts ultimately conclude that their purpose was probably religious.

Relics from prehistoric times at least offer some intriguing names for visitor attractions. *The Hurlers*, north of Liskeard, are said to be named after a group who played hurling (a type of rugby) illegally on a Friday and were therefore transformed to stone. In those days, the calendar was extremely important. South of Penzance are the *Merry Maidens,* a stone circle dated to the late Stone Age about 3,000 to 4,000 years ago, and supposedly depicting a group of 19 girls. According to the legend, a spell was cast on them and they were transformed to stone because they performed a dance here on a Sabbath. Have no fear: you are not subject to these kinds of sanctions today!

# MIF OR TIF?

England is a great nation of tea drinkers and Devon and Cornwall are no exception. The most delicious mealtimes include the little word *tea – high tea, afternoon tea,* and especially in Devon and Cornwall the ubiquitous *cream tea.* A cup of tea and *scone* go together – scones are a kind of crumbly cake served with jam and clotted cream. Breakfast blends from Assam, Ceylon and Kenya are the most popular varieties, and every self-respecting tea drinker will order an Earl Grey, which is supposedly served in royal circles.

What is the correct way to drink tea? Etiquette rules still appear to be sacrosanct in this country, so it is important not to do anything wrong with the nation's favourite beverage. The answer is: opinions are divided between *MIF* and *TIF.* While some prefer to pour milk into the cup first (*milk in first* – MIF), others begin with the tea and then add a drop of milk (*tea in first* – TIF). There are pros and cons on both sides, but personal preference is what counts. One thing is for certain: nobody drinks cream in tea!

Ancient stone circles – always inspire fantastic tales

# LEGENDARY KING

Since the British comedy group Monty Python honoured King Arthur in "Monty Python and the Holy Grail", almost everybody has heard about the legends surrounding the mystic monarch. Tintagel Castle, on the north Cornish coast, is said to be the site of Arthur's conception, and he supposedly lived in all manner of other places, or was seen or rode past them. Not a single piece of evidence confirms that Arthur ever existed. Let alone that his knights ever found the Holy Grail, as it is recorded. It is certain that the present-day ruins of Tintagel Castle didn't exist during Arthur's lifetime. Moreover, the many round tables, around which his knights are said to have congregated, and are proudly presented today, also date to a much later period. It is also equally uncertain whether the area around Glastonbury could be the mythical Avalon where Arthur is said to be buried. Are his mortal remains buried anywhere? Let's wait and see – and maybe enjoy a cup of *Cornish tea*.

# FOOD & DRINK

**Are you a fan of fish and seafood? Then you will love Devon and Cornwall! Cod, lobster, oysters and mussels – fish served here is generally from the local region. You can taste the freshness.**

Fortunately, it's a long time since the bars and restaurants mostly served *fish & chips*. Famous *TV chefs* like Jamie Oliver and Cornwall's masterchef, Rick Stein, have successfully campaigned for *healthy eating*. They've also set an example: chefs in many small country pubs prepare fine quality food. Gastro pub food almost seems like a new type of sport, even in the remotest small pubs.

There is a wide choice, and meat-eaters have plenty of options. Devon and

Cornwall are well known for *steaks and lamb dishes,* as the meat is invariably sourced from local farms where the livestock can graze outdoors all year round. This also makes dairy products exceptional. While lactose-free and soya-based products are widely available, people here generally love *whole milk* from English cows. This makes the ice cream and yoghurts creamier in Devon and Cornwall than elsewhere. Hamburgers are another highly popular gastro food. Fast food chains once dominated the market. In recent years, more and more trendy restaurants have opened selling so-called *posh burgers*, like Byron and Gourmet Burger Kitchen. This is a sign of another British gastro food trend: independent and mainly

## Who says that the English cannot cook? In Devon and Cornwall the cuisine is as creative as in France

*countrywide restaurant chains* have opened here for almost every type of food. The same applies for pubs where the majority of establishments are owned by breweries and pub groups. Local landlords are becoming few and far between, although it is not always obvious.

Traditionally, pubs only served food at lunchtimes – but this has changed in the meantime. More and more pubs offer an extensive dinner menu. Restaurants are usually open from noon to 2.30pm, and from 6.30pm to 9.30pm (last orders). Small restaurants also often close on Mondays.

Britons nowadays are keen on fitness and healthy eating. There are also plenty of options for *vegetarian and vegan* diets on every menu.

Restaurants and pubs offer a variety of options and cater for special dietary requirements. Most menus label those dishes with special ingredients. More expensive restaurants sometimes even offer a separate vegetarian or vegan

# LOCAL SPECIALITIES

**Cornish cheese** – with nearly 60 varieties of cheese produced in Cornwall from Cornish Blue to Brie it's not surprising that Cornish cheeses have won many awards

**Cornish pasty** – traditionally, pastry filled with meat. A vegetarian version of this satisfying snack is now also available

**Crumble** – either with apple (photo left), pear or blackberries: this fruit compote baked with a crumble topping is a classic dessert. Served with custard

**Fish & chips** – deep-fried fish with chips, best with salt and malt vinegar. Often served with mushy peas as well as tartar sauce (photo right). The perfect dish to enjoy beside the seaside

**Plymouth Gin** – its original gin has been distilled using seven exotic botanicals, soft Dartmoor water and pure grain alcohol since 1973. The oldest working gin distillery in England

**Scones** – the scone dough makes delicious cakes, which are often served for afternoon cream tea. First, they are sliced, then filled with jam and clotted cream. The Cornish version is jam first, then the cream. In Devon, the custom is the reverse

**Scrumpy** – a type of cider from Devon. It's made using apples which have fallen off trees before ripening – producing a unique taste

**Stargazey pie** – pies are a way of life in this part of the country. This one consists of small fish (originally pilchards), eggs and potatoes covered in a pastry crust and baked. These days langoustines are often used – but one thing is a must; the heads have to be pointing upwards outside of the pie crust so that they appear to be looking up at the sky

**Squab pie** – originally made with pigeon as the name suggests. Today, this delicious West Country dish contains apples and lamb. In Devon, it is served with clotted cream

menu. Friendly advice is offered everywhere if you have problems with a certain product or ingredient, for example if you need gluten- or lactose-free food or to avoid nuts.

You can also save money by buying

food in the supermarket or finding a good delicatessen: chains such as Waitrose and Marks & Spencer specialise in high quality groceries and now have a network of smaller stores selling mainly *salads, sandwiches, sushi* and fruit selections that compare favourably with restaurants.

The English prefer to drink in pubs. Although wine is widely available in restaurants, beer is still a popular drink. This is also because every size pub rarely offers less than half a dozen different *draught beer varieties*. Large pubs can even offer twice as many different beers. *Lager* is a firm favourite. Popular lagers are international brands like Heineken or Kronenbourg 1664. *Local breweries* now also feature more frequently: St Austell Brewery's Korev lager holds its own against the market power of major competitors. St Ives Brewery also produces a *lager,* as well as Bays from Paignton in Devon.

The popularity of lagers might have suppressed an original British speciality. But in the late 1990s, large pub chains came to the rescue with the campaign for *real ale* – a red beer that lacks carbonation. The beer is drawn at cellar temperature and has become a stalwart choice in pubs. The trend for craft beer has helped especially smaller breweries to have another chance at the beer kegs. As for stouts, the dark, velvety soft beers, Irish Guinness is still the undisputed Number One. However, there are also surprising novelties from local breweries.

Another, much fruitier speciality is pleasant-tasting, although mostly made in the neighbouring county of Somerset: *cider*. This apple beverage contains the same amount of alcohol in Britain as a beer, and numerous different versions are available. If you go to the

Off to the pub: fresh draught beer from the barrel

trouble of trying out other varieties than the usual pub brands, you will find some incredibly *creative ciders* – some are drier, while others are sweeter than usual and they can also be made with entirely different fruits.

# SHOPPING

To describe Devon and Cornwall as a shopping paradise would probably be an exaggeration. But planning a shopping trip here is very easy. In almost every big city, the shops are open on Sundays – at least for some hours. Additionally, there are 24-hour supermarkets and big out-of-town retail parks.

British as well as international fashion stores usually have ubiquitous and familiar chains in pedestrian areas of bigger cities, but independent shops are still open in smaller towns. Plus, the weekly markets are still busy here and offer a good selection of regional food products.

## ANTIQUES

Some people spread the unfair rumour that the whole of Cornwall is antique. But in south-west England you can acquire plenty of vintage items.

Honiton in East Devon is the main centre for antique hunters – there are about two dozen antique shops. Barnstaple is another good place as well as Lostwithiel near St Austell in Cornwall. You can buy crockery and glasses at one of the many flea markets that are common in Devon.

## ART

Talented artists are not only found in the artists' centre in St Ives – many small towns have privately run galleries which showcase works by local artists. Oil and watercolours with coastal motifs are often available – these paintings tend to catch the eye of visitors in holiday mood.

However, souvenirs also come in different forms: coasters with artful designs, tea towels and mugs. Sometimes, you can also discover new and promising talents.

## GARDEN CENTRES

It's not surprising at all that Devon and Cornwall are attractive for amateur gardeners. The big country garden centres offer everything from seeds to flower pots for small balconies as well as for larger gardens.

The National Trust now also has shops at its visitor attractions many of which have a wide assortment of horticultural items. But beware of many plants growing outdoors in southern England: the winter frost back home can quickly kill off the plants.

Shopping with a personal touch: both counties have plenty of small, independent retailers

## GROCERIES

Regional products are particularly important in the region of Devon and Cornwall. It is worthwhile not only shopping in supermarkets but also in the numerous small delicatessens. These often sell homemade jam from the region, sauces, chutneys and much more. The *Cornish Sea Salt Company* produces sea salt from the Lizard Peninsula. Furthermore, approximately 100 different cheese varieties are produced in Devon and Cornwall.

Tea from England is well known, although the tea is usually mainly sourced from Asia, notably from India and Nepal. *Tregothnan* supplies tea, which is grown near Truro. This doesn't apply (yet) for coffee, but there are also some excellent coffee roasteries in southern England, including *DJ Miles* in Porlock (Exmoor).

Several wine-growing estates have opened in recent decades, including *Eastcott* near Okehampton and *Polgoon* near Penzance. Many of them also produce cider. Gin distilleries are popular as well. In addition to classic *Plymouth* gin, there are many smaller producers such as *Elemental* from St Columb.

## SURFWEAR

Bathing and surfwear is widely available in coastal resorts, especially in Newquay. Many items are not necessarily cheaper here, but the choice is wide. *Saltrock* and *Finisterre* are two cool surfwear brands from Cornwall – for all those who are looking for something different from the popular international trends.

# WEST CORNWALL

**West Cornwall could almost be described as Britain's 'sunshine state' and draws crowds of visitors every year.**

The island's westernmost point, Land's End, lies here as well as the most southerly tip at Lizard Point. There are picture book beaches and fascinating rocky coastal areas – the scenery makes the perfect backdrop for films and television series. Therefore, this is a popular film location for many programmes.

At this part of the country, you meet rugged and eccentric characters whose livelihoods are centred outside Great Britain's metropolitan areas. You also meet well-travelled people who have brought back food trends from France,

surfer fashion from Australia, technology from Tokyo and share this by setting up new hotels, small restaurants and beach shops.

Truro is the county's capital – it is a relatively small city that in recent decades has developed into a busy hub. Penzance retains the raw charm of an important fishing port. St Ives is Cornwall's artists' paradise. Newquay on the other hand is among the top surfing spots in Europe. If you have already seen these places, you can set off to explore an offshore group of islands: the Isles of Scilly.

Plenty of sunshine, clear water, exotic plants – if these islands somehow remind you of islands in the Pacific, you are not far off the mark.

Photo: Beach near Bedruthan Steps

The paradise of England: Cornwall's west coast is lined with beaches, crystal-clear water and idyllic spots

# FALMOUTH

(127 E4) (*U E10–11*) **In Cornwall's biggest natural harbour, the tides are still a focal point.**

From Falmouth (pop. 20,000) ferries make the crossing to St Mawes. You can find out more about maritime history in the National Maritime Museum. The town centre also has quaint narrow alleys and Georgian houses. A number of beautiful beaches on the outskirts of Falmouth attract the crowds during the summer.

SIGHTSEEING

### NATIONAL MARITIME MUSEUM

This regional branch of London's National Maritime Museum has a full-scale replica of a Viking ship for visitors to enjoy along with underwater exploration and exciting reports from fishermen of bygone days. The view from the ⚓ look out tower offers sweeping views across

Bring the net and let's get started: young explorers on Falmouth beach

almost everything is prepared with locally sourced produce. *46 Arwenack Street | tel. 01326 2129 97 | www.hunky doryfalmouth.co.uk | Expensive*

### OLIVER'S ✪

This restaurant serves contemporary British cuisine mostly prepared with locally sourced produce. *33 High Street | tel. 01326 2181 38 | www.oliversfalmouth. com | Expensive*

## WHERE TO STAY

### FALMOUTH BAY GUESTHOUSE

Recently refurbished guesthouse in the city centre. *8 rooms | 8 Pennance Road | tel. 01326 3130 41 | www.falmouth-bay. co.uk | Moderate*

### THE ROYAL DUCHY HOTEL ☆

Wonderful luxury boutique hotel by the seaside overlooking the bay. *45 rooms | Cliff Road | tel. 01326 3130 42 | www. royalduchy.co.uk | Expensive*

## INFORMATION

Visitor Information Centre | Prince of Wales Pier | 11 Market Strand | tel. 01326 7411 94 | www.falmouth.co.uk

the harbour. *Daily 10am–5pm | admission £12.50 | Discovery Quay | www. nmmc.co.uk*

### PENDENNIS CASTLE

450 years of history: the old fortress on a rocky headland near the harbour has numerous exhibitions, including a First World War exhibition and Victorian defences. *April–Oct daily, Nov–March Sat/Sun 10am–4pm | admission £8.40 | Castle Drive | www.english-heritage.org.uk*

## FOOD & DRINK

### HUNKYDORY RESTAURANT ✪

Trendy restaurant – every plate is a work of art. Dishes include vegan and meat,

## WHERE TO GO

### ROSELAND & ST MAWES
(127 E–F4) (*ᴍ E10*)

The small fishing port of St Mawes (pop. 850) on the other side of Carrick Roads harbour resembles a smaller copy of the larger city of Falmouth. A network of small alleyways criss-crosses the town which also has a fort: *St Mawes Castle (April–Oct daily, Nov–March Sat/Sun 10am–4pm | admission £5.40 | Castle Drive | www.english-heritage.org.uk).*

The surrounding area is known as the Roseland Peninsula and is popular with wildlife enthusiasts. ⚓ *St Anthony Lighthouse* here is not only one of England's most attractive lighthouses but also accommodates a INSIDER**TIP** *holiday flat (Sally Port Cottage | 2 rooms | St Anthony | Portscatho | tel. 01386 70 11 77 | www.ruralretreats.co.uk | Moderate).* This is a cool place to stopover. *Information: www.stmawes.info*

# ISLES OF SCILLY

**(126 A–B 1–2) (*ω A–B 9–10*) The ★ Isles of Scilly are probably the least familiar part of England. This is not the only reason why they are so interesting.**
The Isles of Scilly (pop. 2,200) lie southwest of Land's End and are so remote from the rest of the British Isles that residents have created a world of their own. The water is crystal clear, as it is in the Pacific, and exotic plants grow everywhere. The sun shines relatively often. The islands offer everything that you need for a relaxing holiday. The only thing missing here is the ordinary hustle and bustle. Travel by plane from Exeter *(only March–Oct)*, Newquay and Land's End *(from £70 each way).* By boat from Penzance *(March–Oct | from £45 each way).* There are cheap ● INSIDER**TIP** day trips *(from £40 return)* by boat or plane, or a combination of both. *Information and bookings: www.islesofscilly-travel.co.uk*

## SIGHTSEEING

### BRYHER
You can walk to the small, rugged island at low tide from Tresco. Bryher offers fabulous opportunities for hiking and snorkelling, as the water here is calmer than near the other islands. INSIDER**TIP** Homemade fudge is available from the farm owned by Kris and Geoff Taylor *(Veronica Farm | www.veronicafarmfudge.co.uk).*

**MARCO POLO HIGHLIGHTS**

## ST AGNES

England's last bastion in the Atlantic – in fact not Land's End, but St Agnes is the westernmost point of Great Britain. The white sandy beaches are beautiful and the rugged green countryside is inviting for a short hike. St Agnes is also home to one of England's smallest farms: INSIDER**TIP** *Troytown Farm (www.troy town.co.uk)* produces delicious ice cream, *clotted cream* and butter with milk from nine Jersey cows.

## ST MARY'S

The biggest island on the Isles of Scilly also has the largest population (1,800 residents). Most essential amenities are in the small capital *Hugh Town* such as shops, banks, restaurants and bicycle hire. A good starting point are the bus tours run by *Island Rover (Mon–Sat 10.15am and 1.30pm | £8 | Lower Strand | tel. 01720 42 21 31 | www.island rover.co.uk)*. The *Boatsmen Association (£9 return | Rose Cottage | The Strand | tel. 01720 42 39 99 | www.scillyboating. co.uk)* offers crossings to other islands – you should check the schedule at the harbour, as it changes daily.

## TRESCO

On St Mary's traffic-free neighbouring island, you can relax on the beach and forget everyday routines, and in the enchanting *Tresco Abbey Garden (daily 10am–4pm | admission £15 | www.tresco. co.uk)* you can find plants from around the world. A small exhibition of shipwrecked figureheads is also well worth a visit.

# LOW BUDGET

Cider is as much a part of Devon and Cornwall as cream teas and Cornish pasties. The carbonated apple drink is available in every pub. ● *Healeys Cornish Cyder Farm (daily 9am–5pm| free admission | Penhallow | Truro | tel. 01872 57 33 56 | www.thecornish cyderfarm.co.uk)* produces the alcoholic beverage. You can enjoy free tours of the farm and sample the cider.

Accommodation in Cornwall is expensive, especially in peak season – but several budget hotel chains have opened – they may all seem uniform but often have exceptionally reasonably priced rooms. The biggest chains are *Travelodge (www.travelodge. co.uk)*, *Premier Inn (www.premierinn. com)* and *Holiday Inn Express (www. ihg.com)*.

## FOOD & DRINK

### FRAGGLE ROCK BAR 🕙

Even the wine here comes from Cornwall and almost everything else is locally grown on the Isles of Scilly. Modern British cuisine prepared with locally sourced produce. *Harbour View | Bryher | tel. 01720 42 22 22 | www.bryher.co | Budget*

### JULIET'S GARDEN 🔆

Delicious British cuisine with breathtaking views across the bay of Hugh Town. *Seaway | Porthlow | St Mary's | tel. 01720 42 22 28 | www.julietsgardenrestaurant. co.uk | Expensive*

## LEISURE & SPORT

The Isles of Scilly make the ideal spot for snorkelling and diving, as about 900 shipwrecks are dotted around the islands. You can try *Scilly Seal*

Exotic plants on a small island in the ocean: Tresco Abbey Garden

Snorkelling (£46 | St Martin's | tel. 01720 42 28 48 | www.scillysealsnorkelling.com). All islands have amazing hiking routes. The fine sandy beaches are also perfect for sunbathing.

## WHERE TO STAY

### SCILLY COUNTRY HOUSE
Self-catering holiday homes next door to a Bavarian cafe. *7 rooms | Sage House | High Lancs | St Mary's | tel. 01720 42 24 40 | www.scillycountryhouse.com | Budget*

### STAR CASTLE HOTEL
Chic hotel located in an old garrison near Hugh Town on St Mary's. *38 rooms | The Garrison | St Mary's | tel. 01720 42 23 17 | www.star-castle.co.uk | Expensive*

## INFORMATION

*Tourist Information Centre | Porthcressa Bank | St Mary's | tel. 01720 42 40 31 | www.visitislesofscilly.com*

# LIZARD

*(127 D–E 5–6) (ill D–E 11–12)* **On the Lizard Peninsula the idyllic scenery is perfect for filming romantic novels.**
Rocky cliff-tops, formed by the waves of the Atlantic Ocean, define this part of Cornwall. Down below you will find the fine sandy beaches and on the cliffs vast stretches of grassland and quaint villages.

## SIGHTSEEING

### KYNANCE COVE
The greenish-brown serpentine stone in this beautiful bay reflects vibrant red hues at sunset. It is well worth a visit at other times of the day too, and you should preferably walk along the

Fine sandy beaches along the rocky coastline are typical for the Lizard Peninsula

impressive coastal path from Lizard Point (3 km/1.9 mi away). There is a wonderful view overlooking the bay from ⁓ *Kynance Café (only March–Oct | Kynance Cove | www.kynancecovecafe. co.uk | Budget). www.nationaltrust.org. uk/kynance-cove*

### LIZARD POINT ★ ⁓

Lizard Point is not only England's southernmost tip, but also a magnificent destination for walking and hiking tours. The white *Lizard Lighthouse (Lizard Village | May–Oct Mon–Thu 11am–5pm | admission £8 | www.trinityhouse.co.uk)* is already visible from afar.

From *Bass Point (Tue, Fri 7–9pm, Sun, May–Sept also Wed, July/Aug also Thu 1.30pm–4.30pm | free admission | www. nationaltrust.org.uk/features/marconi-on-the-lizard)* and only a short walk in an easterly direction, it was in 1900 that the Italian Guglielmo Marconi sent the first radio signals across the Atlantic. The unassuming, intriguing site with cabins still stands today. One of the cabins has been converted to a simple **INSIDER TIP** *holiday cottage (Wireless Cottage | 1 room | tel. 0344 8 00 20 70 (*) | www.nationaltrustholidays.org.uk | Moderate).*

### ST KEVERNE

One of the most photogenic places (pop. 2,100) on The Lizard: the 16th-century church is surrounded on all sides by an attractive network of small houses and numerous palm trees. This is also a place of historic interest: in 1497, the Cornish rebellion was started in St Keverne when residents protested against the king's tax increases. However, the uprising was thwarted. A statue commemorates the event. Just outside the village of

St Keverne is the farm ⊕ INSIDER TIP *Roskilly's (Tregellast Barton Farm | School Hill | www.roskillys.co.uk)* – it is well known for its ice cream and Jersey cow milk.

## FOOD & DRINK

### ANN'S PASTIES
The locals' choice for *Cornish pasties* – a traditional speciality of baked pastry with a beef filling. *Sunny Corner | Beacon Terrace | www.annspasties.co.uk | Budget*

### POLPEOR CAFÉ ⬧⬧
Small café on Lizard Point, slightly touristy, but with fabulous views. *Lizard Point | Budget*

## WHERE TO STAY

### MULLION COVE HOTEL ⬧⬧
A traditional, refurbished hotel in an idyllic coastal setting. Also offers holiday apartments. *30 rooms | Cliff Road | Mullion | tel. 01322 25 02 71 | www.mullion-cove.co.uk | Expensive*

## INFORMATION

*Tourist Information Centre | 79 Meneage Street | Helston | tel. 01326 56 54 31*

## WHERE TO GO

### GODOLPHIN (126 C4) (*M C11*)
This house and country estate dates to Tudor times and looks like a castle that was built rather too flat, with its imposing stone façade and rectangular battlements.
The house is surrounded by a wonderful garden. At the ⬧⬧ south-western end, there is a fantastic view as far as St Ives' bay and the tidal island of St Michael's Mount. *Jan–Oct daily 10am–5pm,* *Nov/Dec 10am–4pm | admission £8.10 | Godolphin Cross | Helston | www.national trust.org.uk/godolphin*

### PORTHLEVEN (127 D5) (*M D11*)
The small fishing port (pop. 3,000) near Helston is a popular spot for photographers waiting for extreme waves. In the harbour, there are small shops and cafés including *Sea Drift (Fore Street | tel. 01326 55 87 33 | www.seadriftporth leven.co.uk | Moderate)* that serves excellent fish and cakes. In the southeast is *Penrose (www.nationaltrust.org. uk/penrose)*, a picturesque stretch of countryside by Cornwall's largest natural lake, *Loe.*
The *Poldark Mine (April–Oct daily, Nov– March Tue, Thu, Sat 10.30am–3pm | admission museum £6.25 with tour £23.60 | Trenear | Wendron | www.pol darkmine.org.uk)* about 10 km/6.2 mi north-east is Cornwall's only underground tin mine that is still open to visitors today.

# NEWQUAY

**(127 E1) (*M E8*) You should not expect too much of a surfers' paradise – except high waves and a perfect beach.**
Newquay (pop. 20,000) is a typical small town with pedestrian area and not the most picturesque spot locally. But the beaches are fantastic.

---

🏙 **WHERE TO START?**
To the **beach**! Park at the station and take a stroll on the opposite side of Cliff Road to Great Western Hotel. The path leads downhill.

---

## FOOD & DRINK

### FIFTEEN ☼

Delicious food by TV chef Jamie Oliver in a unique atmosphere by the beach. *On the Beach | Watergate Bay | tel. 01637 86 10 00 | www.fifteencornwall.co.uk | Expensive*

### THE GRIFFIN INN

Rustic pub with hearty food and excellent *fish & chips. Cliff Road | tel. 01637 87 40 67 | www.griffin-inn-newquay.co. uk | Budget*

## LEISURE & SPORT

The ★ ● beaches at Newquay present picture postcard scenes. That starts in the town's centre at *Great Western Beach*, a wonderful sandy beach along the rocky shoreline. The most popular beaches for surfing and other water sports are *Fistral Beach* and, slightly further away, *Watergate Bay.* This has turned into a trendy spot with fine gastro food. You can hire surf boards and take surfing lessons at the *Extreme Academy (Watergate Bay | tel. 01637 86 08 40 | www.extreme academy.co.uk).*

## WHERE TO STAY

### TRAVELODGE

Although this meets the basic budget hotel standard, ☼ several rooms have INSIDER TIP some of the best sea views that Newquay has to offer. *76 rooms | Cliff Road | tel. 0871 9 84 62 44 (*) | www. travelodge.co.uk | Budget*

### WATERGATE BAY HOTEL ●

Contemporary and luxury spa hotel in an idyllic location on the beach. *69 rooms | Watergate Bay | tel. 01637 86 05 43 | www.watergatebay.co.uk | Expensive*

## INFORMATION

*Tourist Information Centre | Marcus Hill | tel. 01637 83 85 16 | www.visitnew quay.org*

## WHERE TO GO

### BEDRUTHAN STEPS (127 E1) (*Ø E7*)

Cornwall's most spectacular rocky coastline: single rock stacks rise from the sand near the rocky cliff-tops and form a pattern of steps. The legend goes that the giant Bedruthan used them as steps. *St Eval | Bedruthan | www.nationaltrust. org.uk/carnewas-at-bedruthan | 13 km/ 8.1 mi north*

### TRERICE (127 E2) (*Ø E8*)

A fine Elizabethan manor house on the outskirts of Newquay with Dutch façade elements as well as a 300-year-old clock. The adjacent *Barn Restaurant (Budget)* in a converted barn is well known for its INSIDER TIP lemon cake. *March–Oct daily 11am–5pm | admission £9.45 | Kestle Mill | www.nationaltrust.org.uk/trerice | 5 km/3.1 mi south-east*

# PENZANCE

(126 B5) (*Ø B11*) **The smell of the fish and sea hangs in the air in Penzance (pop. 21,000).**

The city at the heart of south-west Cornwall has kept its reputation as a fishing port – more industrious than picturesque. Sardine shoals still run off the coast here. Nearby *Newlyn* continues to be one of the most important fishing ports in Great Britain.

Penzance will probably never earn accolades as one of Great Britain's most beautiful cities, but it has its charms. The main shopping area is Market Jew Street with

St Michael's Mount: not only the name is evocative of Mont-Saint-Michel in France

its 19th-century *Market Building* with impressive dome at the far end.

## SIGHTSEEING

### NEWLYN ART GALLERY

It's hard to believe that this small fishing port once attracted artists from around the world. The *Newlyn School of Arts* was a late Impressionist artists' colony. You can visit another branch of the gallery at *Penlee House* in Penzance. *Tue–Sat, in summer also Mon 10am–5pm | admission £2.20 | New Road | Newlyn | www. newlynartgallery.co.uk*

### ST MICHAEL'S MOUNT ★ ☾

The tidal island of St Michael's Mount offers romantic views, especially at sunrise and sunset, which are similar to those at Mont-Saint-Michel in France. The similarity is no accident: King Edward gifted the small island in the 11th century to the Benedictine monks from Normandy who built a monastery here. You can walk to St Michael's Mount at low tide, while boats and an amphibious vehicle offer transport at high tide. *March–Oct Sun–Fri 10.30am–5.30pm, Nov/Dec and Feb Tue, Fri 10.30am–4pm | admission £14.00 | Marazion | www.stmichaels mount.co.uk*

### TRENGWAINTON GARDEN

Many plants grow in this garden that shouldn't thrive in the British Isles, including magnolias and camellias. The gardeners have brought plants from India and Myanmar to Cornwall. *Feb–Oct Sun–Thu 10.30am–5pm | admission £8.10 | Madron | www.nationaltrust.org. uk/trengwainton-garden*

## FOOD & DRINK

### MACKEREL SKY SEAFOOD BAR

The small bar serves the catch of the day. *Only March–Oct | The Bridge | New Road | Newlyn | tel. 01736 44 89 82 | www.mack erelskycafe.co.uk | Budget*

Crashing waves as a backdrop: the Minack Theatre is a unique open-air stage

## LEISURE & SPORT

### JUBILEE POOL ● ☽

On the promenade – the Art Deco lido pool dating from 1935 was refurbished in 2015 and is now a modern leisure pool. You not only enjoy a large seawater pool but also an amazing view of St Michael's Mount and the artist's village of Newlyn. *May–Sept daily 10.30am–6pm | admission £5 | Promenade | www.jubileepool.co.uk*

## WHERE TO STAY

### LAMORNA COVE HOTEL

Modern self-catering apartments with pool, a short distance from Penzance. *16 rooms | Lamorna Cove | Lamorna | tel. 01736 27 89 90 | www.lamornacovehotel.com | Moderate*

### VENTON VEAN

Small, luxury B&B with boutique style décor. *5 rooms | Trewithen Road | tel. 01736 35 12 94 | www.ventonvean.co.uk | Moderate*

## INFORMATION

*Penzance National Trust Visitor Centre Station Approach | tel. 01736 33 55 30 | www.purelypenzance.co.uk*

## WHERE TO GO

### LAND'S END ● ☽ (126 A5) (⌀ A11)

England's westernmost landmark relies on its unique selling point. There is the country's "First and Last Inn" as well as an interactive exhibition mainly designed for children. The tourist attractions are crowded but there is a spectacular rocky coastline. It is well worth exploring the coastal path. You can stopover in *Land's End Hotel (30 rooms | tel. 01736 87 18 44 | www.landsendhotel.co.uk | Moderate)*, a refurbished hotel on the cliff-top. *Sennen | www.landsend-landmark.co.uk | 15 km/9.3 mi west*

**PORTHCURNO** (126 A5) (*ﾉﾉ B11*)

This picturesque location on the coast with a wonderful sandy beach owes its development to modern telecommunications. At times, up to 14 cables from the US, India and other parts of Europe were laid under the sea. The *Telegraph Museum (April–Oct daily 10am–5pm, Nov–March Sat–Mon 11am–4.30pm | admission £8.95 | Eastern House | www. telegraphmuseum.org)* provides more information. Here, you can now also view a network of INSIDERTIP tunnels – a long-kept secret – that were hewn into the rocks in 1941 to protect against invasion.

The nearby ★ ☆ *Minack Theatre is* an impressive place *(March–Sept daily 9.30am–5pm, Oct–Feb 10am–3.30pm | admission £5 | guided tours in summer, check schedule | Porthcurno Coast | www.minack.com)*: it was built in 1934 high on the cliffs and is Great Britain's oldest open-air theatre. *15 km/9.3 mi south-west*

# ST AUSTELL

(122 C5) (*ﾉﾉ G9*) **It's surprising that St Austell (pop. 34,700) is Cornwall's biggest town: the town centre seems rather small and the major attractions emerged relatively late.**

St Austell was for many centuries a centre for the kaolin (china clay) industry. Tourism has only flourished since the 1990s when the last mines closed in the south-west. You can find out more about the history at the *Wheal Martyn China Clay Heritage Centre (daily 10am–4pm | admission £9.75 | Wheal Martyn | Carthew | www.wheal-martyn. com | 5 km/3.1 mi north)* which is slightly outside the town centre.

## SIGHTSEEING

### CHARLESTOWN

At the end of the 19th century it was important to find a harbour to transport

# EXPLORING CORNWALL'S MINES

Once upon a time, it was often dirty, dark, chilly and damp working in Devon and Cornwall. The mining industry thrived in both counties – there were many tin and copper mines as well as a few silver and zinc mines. Natural resources must have been mined here over 4,000 years ago. Immerse yourself in this past: in *Geevor Tin Mine (2 April–Oct Sun–Fri 9am–5pm, Nov–March 10am–4pm | mine tours in summer from 10am | admission £13.95 | Penwith Heritage Coast | Pendeen | www.geevor. com)* you can go underground and explore the old mines. The pump house

at ☆ *Wheal Coates (free admission | always open | Beacon Drive | St Agnes | www.nationaltrust.org.uk/wheal-coates)* stands like a memorial on Cornwall's north coast – only the walls and a chimney remain, but it makes a fabulous subject for photographs. Many towns, ports and roads were only built due to the mining industry. Ultimately, as is so often the case, the infrastructure was no longer needed. In 1998, when *South Crofty Mine* near Poole closed, the last mine disappeared in the southwest of England. *www.cornish-mining.org.uk*

the kaolin. St Austell developed this port from a small fishing village. Now, this once small village is better known for its role as a backdrop in the filming of Poldark.

The *Shipwreck and Heritage Centre (March–Oct daily 10am–5pm | admission £5.95 | Quay Road | www.shipwreck charlestown.com)* presents exhibitions about the numerous shipwrecks just off the coast.

### ST AUSTELL BREWERY
You can see how some of Cornwall's most important beers are produced here. St Austell Brewery brews various lagers, ales and stouts. *Mon–Sat 9am–6pm | admission £12 | 63 Trevarthian Road | www.staustell breweryvisitorcentre.co.uk*

## FOOD & DRINK

### THE PIER HOUSE ☆☆
Steaks, fish and pies – traditional English fare is served at this pub, which has a fabulous view over Charlestown harbour. *Harbour Front | Charlestown | tel. 01726 6 79 55 | www.pierhousehotel. com | Expensive*

## WHERE TO STAY

### THE CARLYON BAY
Top luxury four-star hotel with spa overlooking the sea. *86 rooms | Sea Road | tel. 01726 8123 04 | www.carlyonbay.com | Expensive*

### CORRAN FARM B&B
For those who like farmhouse holidays: this farm outside St Austell offers rooms and breakfast. *3 rooms | only Feb–Nov | Corran Farm | St Ewe | Mevagissey | tel. 01726 84 21 59 | www.corranfarm.co.uk | Budget*

## INFORMATION

*St Austell Tourist Bay Information Centre | Southbourne Road | tel. 01726 87 95 00 | www.staustellbay.co.uk*

## WHERE TO GO

### EDEN PROJECT ★ ● ⊕
**(122 C5) (*M* G9)**
In the James Bond film "Die Another Day" the hero crossed these vast plastic domes. Like a space ship, they span parts of a former kaolin mine and are the heart of an ambitious project: the world's climatic zones are recreated beneath the domes or biomes. Plants from all over the world grow here. The air humidity and temperatures are partly tropical. The energy is mainly generated by wind and solar farms. On the edge of the site there is a simple but modern **INSIDER TIP** *Youth Hostel (60 rooms | tel. 0345 3 71 95 73 (*) | www.yha.org.uk | Budget)* where you can stopover in refurbished ship containers. *Daily 9.30am–6pm, in winter to 4pm | admission £27.50 (£23.50 if you arrive on foot, by bicycle or with public transport) | Bodelva | Par | www.edenproject.com | 8 km/5 mi north-east*

### LOST GARDENS OF HELIGAN ●
**(122 B5–6) (*M* G9)**
The lost garden is blooming again: the Lost Gardens of Heligan were already cultivated in the 18th century but later became overgrown. That was until the initiator of the Eden Project, Tim Smit, discovered and restored them to their former glory. The site comprises several gardens with different designs. Pineapples even grow in the market garden! *April–Oct daily 10am–6pm, Nov–March 10am–5pm | admission £14.50 | Pentewan | www.heligan.com | 10 km/6.2 mi south*

## MEVAGISSEY (122 C6) (*Ⓜ G9*)

A picturesque fishing village (pop. 2,000): the boats are moored in the harbour, and on both sides of the marina there are narrow streets with small cottages that continue uphill. It's not surprising that the village is well known for its tasty fish dishes, for example, at *Sharksfin (The Quay | tel. 01726 84 29 69 | www.thesharksfin.co.uk | Moderate)* in the harbour. From May to September a ☼ INSIDER TIP small ferry travels several times a day from Mevagissey to Fowey with a superb view of the coastline.

Stunning coastal views are also possible at ☼ *Tremarne Hotel (13 rooms | Polkirt | tel. 01726 84 22 13 | www.tremarnehotel.co.uk | Moderate). 10 km/6.2 mi south*

The best way to quench thirst: a pub in the fishing village of Mevagissey

# ST IVES

(126 C4) (*Ⓜ C10*) **Here, you just have to get creative: St Ives (pop. 11,000) is Cornwall's artists' centre.**

It also has four beaches that are all picture postcard perfect with crystal clear water, cute houses and boats crowded into the harbour. The fine weather also means that people are in a good mood. From the stretch of land ☼ *The Island* you can look back at St Ives. In the mid-19th century more and more artists were enticed into this naturally beautiful region, starting with William Turner. Many of them stayed and opened galleries. A trip with the railway ☼ INSIDER TIP *Scenic Tramway (daily | return from £4 | the trains also travel as far as Penzance | www.greatscenicrailways.co.uk)* is probably the most pleasant approach route to the town. This connects St Erth and St Ives along the coast.

### SIGHTSEEING

### BARBARA HEPWORTH MUSEUM

The former home of sculptor Barbara Hepworth is now a museum. Many of her sculptures are on show as well as photos and sketches. *Daily 10am–4.20pm | admission £7 | A combined ticket for £14.50 also includes admission to other local museums | Barnoon Hill | www.tate.org.uk*

### TATE ST IVES ★ ● ☼

The smaller sister to London's Tate Gallery is right on Porthmeor Beach. Contemporary art is displayed with changing exhibitions. It also features less well-known artists who are associated with St Ives. For those not keen on modern art, there is a fabulous view over St Ives and the beach! *March–Oct daily 10am–5pm, Nov–Feb 10am–4pm | admission £10.50 |*

*Porthmeor Beach | www.tate.org.uk/visit/
tate-st-ives*

### THE BEAN INN 🌱

Vegetarian restaurant also serving plenty of vegan dishes. *Only open in summer | St Ives Road | tel. 01736 79 59 18 | www. thebeaninn.co.uk | Moderate*

### PORTHMEOR BEACH CAFÉ 🌱 🌿

Light snacks and delicious drinks with views of the beach. The ingredients are, whenever possible, sourced from local producers. *Porthmeor Beach | tel. 01736 79 33 66 | www.porthmeor-beach.co.uk | Expensive*

## WHERE TO STAY

### THE BADGER INN

Traditional pub with B&B slightly outside the town centre. *6 rooms | Fore Street | Lelant | tel. 01736 75 21 81 | www.the badgerinn.co.uk | Budget*

### THE GANNET INN

Stylish boutique hotel with adjoining restaurant. *7 rooms | St Ives Road | Carbis Bay | tel. 01736 79 56 51 | www.gannet stives.co.uk | Expensive*

## INFORMATION

*Visit St Ives Information Centre | The Guildhall | Street-An-Pol | tel. 0905 2 52 22 50 (*) | www.stives-cornwall.co.uk*

## WHERE TO GO

### CHUN QUOIT DOLMEN

(126 A4) (*∅ B10*)

About 300 m/328 yards west of *Chun Castle,* the ruins of a hillfort from the Ice Age, an ancient chambered tomb, the Chun Quoit Dolmen, is accessible via a small path. The stones were placed here in the present-day form over 5,500 years ago. *Free admission | turn off Morvah Road between Morvah and Boswarthan | 16 km/9.9 mi west*

# TRURO

(127 E3) (*∅ E9–10*) **In Cornwall, many towns see themselves as small centres but the only genuine capital is Truro (pop. 19,000).**

The centre between Lemon Street and Victoria Square offers something for all shoppers and the city also has several restaurants. Truro only became Cornwall's capital in the 19th century. It was once labelled "Cornwall's London" because of its many impressive Georgian and Victorian buildings. Nowadays, the local people are more modest and Truro is well worth visiting, not only for its strategic central location.

## SIGHTSEEING

### ROYAL CORNWALL MUSEUM

In Cornwall's oldest museum you can discover all the facts about the history of this part of the world, archaeological finds and numerous contemporary artworks that comprise the largest art collection in the county. *Mon–Sat 10am– 4.45pm | admission £5.50 | River Street | www.royalcornwallmuseum.org.uk*

### TRURO CATHEDRAL

The Gothic revival cathedral seems very old like many churches in England – but the building was only finished in 1910. You can enjoy the beautiful choral sounds on weekdays from 5.30pm at ● *Choral Evensong*. On the south side are the remains of St Mary's Church that made way for the new building. *Mon–Sat 7.30am–6pm, Sun 9am–5pm | free admission | 14 St Mary's Street | www.trurocathedral.org.uk*

## FOOD & DRINK

### BUSTOPHER JONES
In the beautifully restored loft-style bistro you can enjoy delicious fish and meat dishes as well as vegetarian food. *62 Lemon Street | tel. 01872 43 00 00 | www.bustopher-jones.co.uk | Expensive*

### THE CORNISH VEGAN ☺
A vegan restaurant in a central location with fabulous creative food. *15 Kenwyn Street | tel. 01872 27 15 40 | www.thecornishvegan.com | Moderate*

## WHERE TO STAY

### THE ALVERTON
A former convent which has been beautifully restored to a stylish hotel. *50 rooms | Tregolls Road | tel. 01872 27 66 33 | www.thealverton.co.uk | Expensive*

### THE VICTORIA INN
Friendly pub with comfortable B&B rooms on the outskirts of Truro. *4 rooms | Chyvelah Road | Threemilestone | tel. 01872 27 83 13 | www.thevicinn.com | Moderate*

## INFORMATION

*Truro Tourist Information Centre | Municipal Buildings | Boscawen Street | tel. 01872 27 45 55 | www.visittruro.org.uk*

## WHERE TO GO

### TRELISSICK GARDEN ❧
(127 E3–4) (*𝄞 E10*)
The estate on the peninsula in the Fal River estuary offers 12 ha/30 acres of countryside with panoramic views. Gingkos, rhododendron, camellias and much more grow here. Many of the plants were reproduced on the porcelain that the Copeland family, the former owners of Trelissick, produced in their factory. Their magnificent country house is also open to visitors. *March–Oct daily 10.30am–5.30pm (house and garden), Nov–Feb 10.30am–4.30pm (garden only) | admission £10.90 (parking extra £4) | Feock | www.nationaltrust.org.uk/trelissick | 8 km/5 mi south*

Acoustic space for beautiful sounds: Truro Cathedral

# EAST CORNWALL

You will discover mystic Cornwall on the east coast: here, you will see ruins and prehistoric legacies. And King Arthur's legend also lingers over some of the sights.

He was reputedly conceived in Tintagel, which is only a legend, but an entire region thrives on this rumour.

Small, enchanted villages are dotted amidst the green and partially wild countryside. Time seems to have stood still in the little ports hidden along the coast. There was a good reason for this: many of the harbours were built to transport natural resources, but trading stopped many years ago. The locals made the best of this: today, they earn their living with authentic restaurants, tiny shops and cosy hotels. While stand-ards may not always conform to metro-politan hotels, the sea views more than compensate.

# BODMIN

*(122 C3–4) (♔ G8)* **For a while in the 19th century, Bodmin (pop. 15,000) was the capital city of Cornwall. This partly explains the many ostentatious buildings that have been preserved until today.**

In the 6th century, St Petroc established a monastery that laid the foundations for the modern town. Little remains of the monastery now and the church that was named after him only dates to the 15th century.

Rugged charm: in East Cornwall you can explore the medieval ruins, secluded harbours and plenty of myths

## SIGHTSEEING

### BODMIN JAIL

The old partial ruins of the former jail are now a tourist attraction. You don't even have to be enthusiastic about the history of executioners and prisoners to join a discovery tour here – the dismal building complex is well worth a visit for everyone. Another interesting historical fact: during the Second World War, the crown jewels were stored here for safekeeping. *Daily 9.30am–6pm |* *admission £10 | Berrycoombe Road |* *www.bodminjail.org*

### CORNWALL'S REGIMENTAL MUSEUM

This military museum, which is housed in "The Keep" displays the history and military equipment of the region's army – mainly military uniforms, medals and weapons. *March–Oct Mon–Sat 10am–5pm, Nov–Feb Tue–Sat 10am–4pm |* *admission £6 | Castle Canyke Road |* *www.cornwalls-regimentalmuseum.org*

Big ideas: Bodmin Moor. Daphne du Maurier also visited here

## FOOD & DRINK

### LANIVET INN

Rustic pub with a wide menu choice, including vegetarian dishes. *Truro Road | tel. 01208 83 12 12 | Moderate*

**INSIDER TIP** WOODS CAFÉ

Its beautiful location is hidden away on the edge of woodland by a stream. The café serves delicious homemade light snacks and cakes, all freshly prepared. *Callywith Cottage | Cardinham Woods | tel. 01208 7 81 11 | www.woodscafecornwall.co.uk | Moderate*

## WHERE TO STAY

### LANHYDROCK HOTEL & GOLF CLUB

This modern hotel in a peaceful setting greets guests with excellent cuisine and wonderful views. *44 rooms | Lostwithiel Road | tel. 0120 26 25 70 | www.lanhydrockhotel.com | Expensive*

## INFORMATION

*Tourist Information Centre | Crinnicks Hill | tel. 01208 7 66 16 | www.bodminlive.com*

## WHERE TO GO

### BODMIN MOOR
(123 D–E 2–3) (*H–J7*)

While everybody heads for Dartmoor, they overlook the equally impressive, smaller Bodmin Moor. It also boasts beautiful hiking trails and fabulous views. Daphne du Maurier was inspired in the guesthouse *Jamaica Inn (rooms available | Bolventor | tel. 01566 8 62 50 | www.jamaicainn.co.uk | Moderate)* to write the novel of the same name that was later filmed by Alfred Hitchcock. There is also a small museum *(daily 8am–9pm | admission £3.95)*, where you can learn more about the 300-year history of smugglers in this region. In the south-eastern region of the moor are the *Hurlers Stone Circles (dawn to dusk | admission free |*

Minions | Liskeard | www.english-herit
age.org.uk) three of the best-preserved
stone circles in the south of England.
The legend states that they were all men
who were turned to stone because they
played Hurling on the Sabbath.

### LANHYDROCK (122 C4) (*∅ G8*)

The magnificent old country house is
in the heart of an enchanted wooded
estate and parkland. The library contains a book that is supposed to have
helped Henry VIII with the annulment
of his first marriage and thus was partly instrumental in the establishment of
the Anglican Church. *House March–Oct
daily 11am–5.30pm, Nov Sat/Sun and
Dec daily 11am–4pm, park dawn to dusk
| admission £13.55 | www.nationaltrust.
org.uk/lanhydrock | 4 km/2.5 mi south*

### RESTORMEL CASTLE ⋇
### (122 C4) (*∅ G8*)

The circular shell-keep of Restormel
Castle, one of Cornwall's best preserved
Norman castles, is in a beautiful setting
on a hilltop by the River Fowey. Although
the site is now a ruin, the outlook clearly
indicates the former strategic importance of this location. *March–Oct Daily
10am–4pm | admission £4.30 | Restormel
Road | Lostwithiel | www.english-heritage.
org.uk | 12 km/7.5 mi south*

# FOWEY

(123 D5) (*∅ H9*) **Every August, thousands of visitors are attracted to
the Fowey Regatta in the small port
(pop. 2,400), but Fowey also has plenty
more to offer.**

The port was once one of the region's
most important shipping centres for the
transport of natural resources. Today,
the town has many fine restaurants and
expensive shops. There are picturesque
panoramic coastal views from the banks
of Fowey River and the small houses on
the hilltops. The writer Daphne du Maurier lived for many years at her *Menabil-
ly estate (not open to the public)* near
Fowey and immortalised it in her novel
"Rebecca". In memory of the writer, the
town has the small Daphne du Maurier Literary Centre and in May holds an
annual INSIDERTIP Festival of Arts and
Literature.

## SIGHTSEEING

### ST CATHERINE'S CASTLE ⋇

The 15th-century St Catherine's Castle is
still relatively well preserved thanks to its
role in the Second World War. The strategic position at the mouth of the River
Fowey estuary served as an anti-aircraft
post. The view of Fowey and the sea from
here is wonderful. *Dawn to dusk | free*

---

★ **Gribbin Head**
Headland with a fantastic
coastal hiking path → p. 52

★ **Calstock Viaduct**
The spectacular railway bridge
over the River Tamar → p. 54

★ **The Seafood Restaurant**
TV chef Rick Stein showcases
his talent here → p. 56

★ **Port Isaac**
Picturesque fishing village which
often features in films → p. 56

★ **Tintagel Castle**
With or without King Arthur:
this castle ruin on the coast is
an adventure → p. 58

**MARCO POLO HIGHLIGHTS**

admission | St Catherine's Cove | www.
english-heritage.org.uk

## FOOD & DRINK

**THE GALLEON INN**
Hearty British pub food. *12 Fore Street |
tel. 01726 83 30 14 | Moderate*

**SAM'S**
Popular burger and fish restaurant
serving excellent food. *20 Fore Street |
tel. 01726 83 22 73 | www.samscornwall.
co.uk | Moderate*

## WHERE TO STAY

**INSIDER TIP ▶ FOWEY HOTEL** ☼
The comfortable rooms offer wonderful
views over the river estuary. The window

# LOW BUDGET

Sightseeing can be expensive, especially the historic attractions. Once
a year, the owners of several thousand British palaces, castles, churches and other buildings invite visitors
free of charge: in early September
watch out for the ● Heritage Open
Days (www.heritageopendays.org.uk).

The days of 20-bunk dorms are
long gone in English youth hostels.
The Youth Hostels Association *YHA*
(www.yha.org.uk) has invested
considerably in recent years: dorms
are available from £15, while a
double room costs from £29. In
Devon and Cornwall, the YHA owns
a number of hostels, including
one at Land's End, Tintagel and
Okehampton.

tables in the restaurant also enjoy fabulous views, if you only want to dine here.
*37 rooms | Esplanade | tel. 01726 8 32 55 |
www.thefoweyhotel.co.uk | Expensive*

## INFORMATION

Tourist Information Centre | Daphne Du
Maurier Literary Centre | 5 South Street |
tel. 01726 83 36 16 | www.fowey.co.uk

## WHERE TO GO

**GRIBBIN HEAD ★** ☼
(122 C5) (*Ⅲ G9*)
As you walk along this headland, south-
west of Fowey, the fresh sea wind blows
in your face. The white and red *Gribbin
Tower at a height of* 26 m/85.3 ft is a
notable landmark and pinpoint for mariners. From here you can enjoy panoramic
sea views. *7 km/4.4 mi south-west*

**POLRUAN** (123 D5) (*Ⅲ H9*)
Polruan (pop. 600) is rather overshad-
owed by Fowey, but it is just as interesting. You can reach the small village on
the other side of the River Fowey by tak-
ing the pleasant *ferry crossing (May–Sept
Mon–Sat 7.15am–11pm, Sun 9am–11pm,
Oct–April Mon–Sat 7.15am–7pm, Sun
10am–5pm | £2 | depending on sched-
uled times, from Whitehouse Pier or Town
Quay | www.ctomsandson.co.uk/polruan-
ferry). Blockhouse Fort (dawn to dusk |
free admission)* is almost a counterpart
to St Catherine's Castle, though not as
well preserved. The same applies to the
ruins of the 8th-century ☼ *St Saviours
Church* that sits majestically above the
village. Well-equipped, modern self-
catering cottages are situated in the har-
bour *Polruan Dream Cottages (4 rooms |
68 West Street | tel. 07711 48 99 00 | www.
polruandreamcottages.co.uk | Moderate).
500 m/1600 ft east*

# LAUNCESTON

**(123 E1–2) (*ꭥ J6*) The centre of Launceston (pop. 11,700) has some impressive buildings for a good reason.**
Until the 19th century, the town was Cornwall's capital city. The small shopping streets around the High Street, Broad Street and Church Street are ideal for window shopping.

## SIGHTSEEING

### LAUNCESTON CASTLE ⭒⭒
This ruined castle dates to the 11th century and is said by some to be a sign of the temporary demise of the British monarchy. In 1973, this was the very place where Prince Charles was proclaimed Duke of Cornwall. *April–Sept daily 10am–6pm, Oct 10am–5pm | admission £4.30 | Castle Lodge | www.english-heritage.org.uk*

### LAWRENCE HOUSE
This elegant museum in a Georgian townhouse presents the history of the town. It also sheds light on the connection to Launceston in Tasmania, which dates from the first departure of British prisoners to Australia. Philip Gidley King from Lawrence was a young Captain who sailed with the first fleet, but he stayed in Australia and later became Governor of New South Wales. *April–Oct Mon–Fri 10.30am–4.30pm | free admission | 9 Castle Street | www.lawrencehousemuseum.org.uk*

## FOOD & DRINK

### JERICHO'S
Enjoy deliciously prepared burgers and steaks in a relaxed atmosphere. *4 Northgate Street | Liberty House | tel. 01566 77 00 80 | www.jerichoskitchen.co.uk | Moderate*

Landmark with eye-catching stripes: the white and red Gribbin Tower

### NUMBER EIGHT ✪
The café serves hot food and lunches prepared with locally sourced ingredients. *8 Westgate Street | tel. 01566 77 73 69 | www.no8launceston.co.uk | Budget*

## WHERE TO STAY

### ROSE COTTAGE B&B ⭒⭒
Beautiful Bed & Breakfast accommodation with wonderful views. *3 rooms | 5 Lower Cleaverfield | tel. 01566 77 92 92 | www.rosecottagecornwall.co.uk | Budget*

## INFORMATION

*Tourist Information Centre | White Hart Arcade | Broad Street | tel. 01566 77 23 21 | www.visitlaunceston.co.uk*

Hang out and dream of adventures: Polperro was once a haven for smugglers

## WHERE TO GO

**TAMAR VALLEY** (123 F2–3) (*[\] K7*)

Much of the river valley extends along the border between Devon and Cornwall and is one of the most beautiful areas for hiking and cycling tours in this part of England.

The Tamar Valley was once a mining region. But the mines have closed and the area has been discovered by weekend day-trippers. One of the most impressive sights is the ★ *Calstock Viaduct* near the village of Calstock. At a height of 37 m/121.4 ft the viaduct is also a railway bridge high above the river.

You can stopover in luxurious accommodation with fine countryside views ⋇ *Endsleigh Hotel (16 rooms | Milton Abbot | tel. 01822 87 00 00 | www.hotel endsleigh.com | Expensive). Information: www.welovethetamarvalley.co.uk | 25 km/15.5 mi south*

# LISKEARD

(123 E4) (*[\] J8*) **Liskeard (pop. 9,000) may not be Cornwall's most attractive town, but it is certainly characteristic of this region.**

Its wealth was generated from the region's copper mines. Nowadays, it has become a commercial centre – and one of the few places where the *Cattle Market (2 Fairpark Road)* is still held every two weeks on Tuesdays. The *Guildhall Clock Tower* soars above the other typical Georgian buildings. The picturesque *Liskeard and Looe Union Canal,* which was built in the 19th century for the mining industry, was closed again in 1910. Now, hiking groups are attracted to the locks that have partly fallen into disrepair.

## SIGHTSEEING

### STUART HOUSE

This medieval town house is conserved by a trust and as well as hosting cultural events in the upstairs rooms it has a small museum with an exhibition about the English Civil War. *Mon–Fri 9.30am–3.30pm, Sat 9.30am–12.30pm | free admission | Barras Street | www.stuart house.org.uk*

## FOOD & DRINK

### HUB CAFÉ ☻

Simple café in a community centre with exclusively vegetarian and vegan food. *Liskerrett Community Centre | Varley Lane | tel. 01579 34 03 07 | Budget*

### INSIDER TIP OLIVE & CO.

Attractive small café in the town centre offering hot snacks. Cosy and serves fresh, homemade food. *Windsor Place | tel. 0794 8 82 80 65 | www.olivecocafe. com | Moderate*

## WHERE TO STAY

### PENCUBITT HOUSE

This country hotel looks like a small castle. Rooms with simple decor and a relaxed atmosphere. *9 rooms | Lamellion Cross | tel. 01579 34 26 94 | www.pencu bitt.com | Moderate*

## INFORMATION

*Tourist Information Centre | Foresters Hall | 1 Pike Street | tel. 01579 34 91 48 | www.visitliskeard.co.uk*

## WHERE TO GO

### LOOE ☆

(123 E5) (*ⓜ J9*)

You can take the INSIDER TIP *Looe Valley Line (£4.30 per trip, day ticket from £4.40 | www.gwr.com)* and travel by train through the beautiful countryside to Looe. The nice coastal town with harbour (pop. 5,300) on Cornwall's southern coast lies on both sides of the River Looe. The town offers many more shops than might be expected from a place of this size.

Rooms with an ocean view are available in the ☆ *Fieldhead Hotel (14 rooms | Portuan Road | Hannafore | tel. 01503 26 26 89 | www.fieldheadhotel.co.uk | Moderate). 14 km/8.7 mi south*

### POLPERRO

(123 D5) (*ⓜ H9*)

If you would like to find out how Polperro (pop. 5,300) became a smuggler's paradise you should visit the local Heritage Museum of *Smuggling and Fishing (April–Oct daily 10.30am–4.30pm | admission £2 | Harbour Studio | The Warren)* in the harbour. The village still feels like a typical fishing port even though fishing is no longer the main activity and tourism has taken over this role. *22 km/13.7 mi south*

### TRETHEVY QUOIT

(123 E3) (*ⓜ J7*)

The 5,500-year-old dolmen, a table-top style tombstone, is also known as *Giant's House*. A stone slab measuring 2.7 m/8.9 ft high is held up by five other standing stones. It is on a much smaller scale than Stonehenge, though just as impressive. *Dawn to dusk | free admission | B3254 near Darite | www. english-heritage.org.uk | 5 km/3.1 mi north*

# PADSTOW

**(122 B3) (*m F7*) If you could create an enchanted spot by a harbour, it would probably look like Padstow (pop. 3,000).** The harbour is enclosed by small houses on three sides and the town centre, nestled behind the hill, has winding alleys and narrow streets. This town is for foodies: TV chef Rick Stein lives in Padstow for part of the year. He also owns about a dozen pubs, hotels and restaurants. This is Cornwall's centre for exceptional fish cuisine. Every year on 1 May, the town celebrates the INSIDER TIP *Obby Oss Festival* with plenty of dancing, music and, of course, food.

## SIGHTSEEING

### QUAYSIDE
This is the hub for Padstow's rather peaceful and quiet life. Fishermen still put out to sea from the quayside. The *Padstow Rock Ferry (daily 8am–5pm, in summer until 8pm | per trip £4 | www. padstow-harbour.co.uk)* operates all year between the harbour and the opposite bank of the River Camel.

### PRIDEAUX PLACE
Every corner of this house is magnificent: Prideaux Place is a manor with elegant interiors and traditional wood panelling. The owners still live here, so opening times are limited. The wonderful parkland is home to one of England's oldest herds of stags. *April–Sept Sun–Thu 12.30pm–4pm | admission £8.50 | Tregirls Lane | www.prideauxplace.co.uk*

## FOOD & DRINK

### THE SEAFOOD RESTAURANT ★
Probably the best restaurant in England as far as fish and seafood are concerned.

Many of the dishes served at Rick Stein's restaurant were swimming in the sea just a short while before. *Riverside | tel. 01841 53 27 00 | www.rickstein.com | Expensive*

### STEIN'S FISH & CHIPS
The cheaper version of Stein's fine cuisine: in this restaurant, you can enjoy *fish & chips. South Quay | tel. 01841 53 27 00 | Moderate*

## SHOPPING

It's incredible how many fashion boutiques there are in this small town! They are mainly on the westside of the harbour in *Church Lane* and *Cross Street*.

## WHERE TO STAY

### OLD CUSTOM HOUSE
A stylish and modernised hotel and pub on the quayside. *24 rooms | South Quay | tel. 01841 53 23 59 | www.oldcustom housepadstow.co.uk | Moderate*

### INSIDER TIP ST PETROC'S HOTEL
You can hardly avoid Rick Stein in Padstow: he developed a blueprint for a boutique hotel with this luxury accommodation. *10 rooms | New Street | tel. 01841 53 27 00 | www.rickstein.com/stay/ st-petrocs-hotel | Expensive*

## INFORMATION

*Tourist Information Centre | North Quay | tel. 01841 53 34 49 | www.padstowlive.com*

## WHERE TO GO

### PORT ISAAC ★ (122 B2) (*m G7*)
A charming fishing village – this is probably why Port Isaac (pop. 700) repeatedly features as a backdrop for films and television series. Down the centuries,

Padstow quayside: pure relaxation and excellent fish cuisine

the village was a relatively important harbour for the local quarries. Nowadays, it has become a tourist centre. Its narrow lanes, which wind their way to the waterside, are perfect for atmospheric photos. You can enjoy a *cream tea* in an original setting, a former chapel, at ● *Chapel Café (Port Isaac Pottery | Roscarrock Hill | tel. 01208 88 13 00 | Budget)*. Accommodation with fabulous sea views: ※ *Morningside B&B (2 rooms | 5 Tintagel Terrace | tel. 01208 88 05 46 | Budget)*. 26 km/15.2 mi north-east

## ROCK AND POLZEATH
(122 B2–3) (*∅ F7*)

On the other side of the River Camel is the small village of INSIDER TIP *Rock* (pop. 1,200). Its nickname is "Chelsea-on-Sea", after London's elegant district, and it is a popular though rather exclusive destination for day trips. This is evident from the fine cuisine. However, Rock's original attraction was its long beach and numerous water sports activities: sailing, surfing, water-skiing and canoeing – everything is possible. Nearby is the district of *Polzeath* whose flat beach attracts visitors from across the county – especially surfers. The surf is usually excellent here. For luxury and chic accommodation look no further than the *St Enodoc Hotel (19 rooms | Rock | tel. 012 08 7 86 33 94 | www.enodoc-hotel.co.uk | Expensive)*. 2 km/1.2 mi east

# TINTAGEL

(122 C1) (*∅ G6*) **A small village (pop. 700) which mainly thrives because of an old legend: King Arthur was supposedly conceived here at Tintagel Castle.**

The monarch earned victory for the Britons in so many battles – at least, according to the legends. But scholars

Not many walls, but plenty of steps and a fabulous outlook: Tintagel Castle

state as a traditional house where you can see what life was like in the Middle Ages. *March–Sept daily 10.30am–5.30pm, Feb and Oct 11am–4pm | admission £4 | Fore Street | short.travel/cod7*

### TINTAGEL CASTLE ★ ☼

This castle is the best evidence for Arthur never having been born – at least not here: it dates to the 13th century and the legends of King Arthur date from the 5th century. Today, only the ruins remain of Tintagel Castle, but it is in a unique setting. You reach a rocky headland over a narrow bridge and can visit the ruins of the iconic castle. The view more than compensates for the numerous steps to climb. *April–Sept daily 10.30am–5.30pm, March and Oct Wed–Sun 10am–4pm, Nov–Feb Sat/Sun 10am–4pm | admission £8.40 | Castle Road | short.travel/cod8*

## FOOD & DRINK

**INSIDERTIP CHARLIE'S CAFÉ AND RESTAURANT**
Excellent restaurant in the centre: burgers, sandwiches and a good breakfast. *Fore Street | tel. 01840 77 95 00 | www.charlies.cafe | Moderate*

**THE CORNISH BAKERY**
A wonderful small café on the way to the castle. Cornish pasties, Danish pastries and excellent coffee. *1a Castle Road | Budget*

## SHOPPING

*Cornish Clotted Cream Gin* is an unusual souvenir and is produced at the local *Wrecking Coast Distillery (The Old Bookshop | Atlantic Road | www.thewreckingcoastdistillery.com):* the gin has a gentle flavour with a hint of juniper and is available in several shops in Tintagel.

are almost convinced that the king may never have existed! There is no real evidence to support his legendary influence. But that makes no difference in Tintagel. The town is busy, if the bus loads of visitors are anything to go by. They arrive here all year to embark on the trail of the fabled king. An adventure tour is handsomely rewarded in this location: the impressive countryside offers one of the most rugged sections of coastline in southern England.

## SIGHTSEEING

### OLD POST OFFICE
For a long time Tintagel's post office was housed in the 14th century farmhouse of the same name. The National Trust has now restored the premises to its former

## WHERE TO STAY

**AVALON HOTEL**
Stylish guesthouse with small rooms. *7 rooms | Atlantic Way | tel. 01840 77 01 16 | www.theavalonhotel.co.uk | Moderate*

**CAMELOT CASTLE HOTEL** ⚜
Enjoy a stopover like a lord of the manor and admire the views of Tintagel Castle. *64 rooms | Atlantic Road | tel. 01840 77 02 02 | www.camelotcastle.com | Moderate*

## INFORMATION

*Tourist Information Centre | Bossiney Road | tel. 01840 77 90 84 | www.visit boscastleandtintagel.com*

## WHERE TO GO

**BOSCASTLE** (122 C1) *(𝄜 G6)*
Boscastle (pop. 800) lies in a romantic valley setting on the confluence of the River Valency and other rivers. In 2004, there was a disastrous flood in this area. Things have now returned to normal. Old houses flank both riverbanks and the harbour nestles into the hillsides almost like an open-air theatre. Legends once circulated about witches and myths, and these are presented in the small *Museum of Witchcraft and Magic (April–Oct Mon–Sat 10.30am–6pm, Sun 11.30am–6pm | admission £5 | www. museumofwitch craftandmagic.co.uk)*. You can stopover at the comfortable pub that serves food: *Wellington Hotel (14 rooms | The Harbour | tel. 01840 25 02 02 | Moderate)*. *6 km/3.7 mi north-east*

**BUDE** (118 A5) *(𝄜 H4–5)*
The small village (pop. 7,700) in the extreme north of Cornwall is popular because of its beaches, including traditional brightly coloured beach huts. In *Bude Castle (April–Oct daily 10am–5pm, Nov.–March 10am–4pm | free admission | The Castle | www.thecastlebude. org.uk)* there is an interesting exhibition of the history of this region, its geology and the shipwrecks off the coast. There is also an art gallery. The *Falcon Hotel (29 rooms | Breakwater Road | tel. 01288 35 20 05 | www.falconhotel.com | Moderate)* has a wonderful riverside location. *30 km/18.6 mi north*

# FOR BOOKWORMS AND FILM BUFFS

**Notes from a Small Island** – (1999) The personal experiences of journalist Bill Bryson during a visit to England. Extremely witty and with a sequel ("It's teatime, my dear", 2017).

**Jamaica Inn** – (1936) An impressive pirates' novel that Daphne du Maurier is said to have written during a stay at Jamaica Inn on Bodmin Moor.

**Poldark** – (2015) Acclaimed TV family drama set in Cornwall in the 18th and 19th century. The television series was based on a novel by Winston Graham.

**Murder Ahoy!** – (1964) One of the legendary Miss Marple films with Margaret Rutherford, filmed in St Mawes. Much of the scenery is exactly the same today.

# SOUTH DEVON

Dartmoor's moorland, small harbour towns like Dartmouth and the busy capital city Exeter – South Devon is a versatile and unique region in the south-west. Plymouth is not only the county's largest city but a maritime centre for the entire country. Famous sailors like Sir Francis Drake put to sea from Plymouth and settlers departed from this port to start a new life in the US. The Royal Navy still has one of its most strategic ports here. Dartmoor thrives on its myths, crime stories and legends, but it is primarily a fabulous region for hiking with some dreamy villages and historical relics. Other visitors are attracted by the beaches: Torquay has several and is regarded as the "English Riviera" with palm trees and warm temperatures.

# DARTMOOR

(124–125 B–D 1–4) (*N L–N 6–8*) **Sherlock Holmes was the famous detective of this region and Edgar Wallace made this the backdrop for his crime stories. ★ Dartmoor, Devon's unique and in many parts isolated moorland, is almost made for detective thrillers.**

There are many myths associated with this national park with its narrow, single-track roads and few passing places that make driving hazardous. However, the countryside and its many impressive sights is inviting for hikers and photographers. Tiny villages like popular Widecombe-in-the-Moor are hidden away, while imposing stone formations

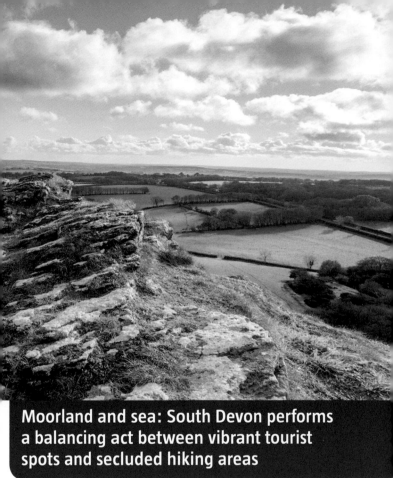

Moorland and sea: South Devon performs a balancing act between vibrant tourist spots and secluded hiking areas

such as Hound Tor offer inspiration for new stories.

## SIGHTSEEING

### CASTLE DROGO ✲

The last castle to be built in Great Britain is more contemporary than it first appears. Building work for this medieval style castle only began in 1910 and continued until 1930. Its impressive position high above the Teign Valley is visible from a distance. It is fully furnished and artists have redesigned some of the rooms. *March–Oct daily 11am–5pm, Nov/Dec Sat/Sun 11am–4pm, countryside dawn to dusk | admission £11 | Drewsteignton (near Exeter) | www.nationaltrust.org.uk/castle-drogo*

### HOUND TOR ✲

There are plenty of tales surrounding the eye-catching stone formations north of Widecombe that were formerly the site of a medieval village – these stories even predate the filming of actor Benedict

In spring thousands of bluebells flower on Dartmoor's green moors

Lydford village you can view the ruins of a small castle: *Lydford Castle (dawn to dusk | free admission | www.english-heritage. org.uk). April–Sept daily 10am–5pm, Oct 10am–4pm, Nov/Dec 11am–3.30pm | admission £8.90 | entrance at the west end of Lydford Village | www.nationaltrust.org. uk/lydford-gorge*

### WIDECOMBE-IN-THE-MOOR

This picturesque village (pop. 600) in the heart of Dartmoor, nestled among hills and moorland, emerged as a collection of small stone cottages around *St Pancras Church.* The writer Beatrice Chase is buried in the old cemetery. The National Trust runs a small shop in *Church House (daily 10.30am–4.30pm)*, formerly a brewery and later a school. *www.wide combe-in-the-moor.com*

## FOOD & DRINK

### CAFÉ ON THE GREEN

Ideal spot for lunch and *afternoon tea.* The large café is in the centre of Widecombe. Enjoy al fresco dining in summer. *The Green | Newton Abbot | Widecombe in the Moor | tel. 01364 621720 | www. thecafeonthegreen.co.uk | Budget*

### THE CLEAVE PUBLIC HOUSE

In this thatched pub in the middle of Dartmoor you can enjoy hearty British food from fish to steak as well as vegetarian options. *Lustleigh | tel. 01647 277223 | www.thecleavelustleigh.co.uk | Moderate*

## WHERE TO STAY

### BOVEY CASTLE

This five-star hotel, built in 1907, on the site of a vast golf course was never a real castle, although it still looks like one. Luxury accommodation in a relaxing setting. *63 rooms | North Bovey | Newton Abbot |*

Cumberbatch, the star of the TV series "Sherlock". The unusual formation is said to be a pack of dogs that were turned to stone by witches. The 6 m/19.7 ft high granite rock, known as *Bowerman's Nose (6 km/3.7 mi north)*, is said to be the hunter.

### LYDFORD GORGE

The gorge continues for 2.4 km/1.5 mi through woodlands in the heart of south-west England. You can explore it on a 5 km/3.1 mi circular trail, which is steep and narrow in certain parts (hiking boots are essential!). The highlight is *White Lady Waterfall* with a 30 m/98.4 ft drop where the River Burn cascades into the River Lyd. In May, a sea of *bluebells* transforms the gorge into a blue oasis. In

*tel. 01647 44 50 00 | www.boveycastle. com | Expensive*

## MITCHELCROFT BED & BREAKFAST
The romantic B&B in south Dartmoor offers rooms with a private terrace, table and chairs. *3 rooms | Scorriton | Buckfastleigh | tel. 01364 63 13 36 | www.mitch elcroft.co.uk | Moderate*

### INFORMATION

*Dartmoor National Park Visitor Centre | Tavistock Road | Princetown | tel. 01822 89 04 14 | www.visitdartmoor.co.uk*

### WHERE TO GO

**OKEHAMPTON** (124 B1) *(ⓜ L5)*
The small town of Okehampton (pop. 7,000) with attractive old houses is one of the centres on the edge of Dartmoor. The 11th-century ruins of *Okehampton Castle (April–Oct daily 10am–5pm | admission £4.80 | Castle*

*Lodge | www.english-heritage.org.uk)* on a wooded spur are mostly incomplete, yet still well worth a visit. A wonderful cycle route on an old railway track is mainly traffic-free INSIDER TIP *Granite Way* from Okehampton railway station extends for 18 km/11.2 mi to Meldon Viaduct. *Bicycle hire: Granite Way Cycle Hire | Klondyke Road | Okehampton | tel. 01837 65 09 07*

# DARTMOUTH

**(125 E5)** *(ⓜ O9)* **The best view of Dartmouth (pop. 5,000) is from the river. Small houses are packed along the river banks, while boats bob up and down in the harbour all year round.**

For centuries, this was one of the country's major deep water ports. Dartmouth has been a Royal Navy base since the 14th century. Officers are still trained here today, and the magnificent *Britannia Royal Naval College* sits majestically above the town.

### MARCO POLO HIGHLIGHTS

⭐ **Dartmoor**
Isolation, heather moors and a perfect crime thriller atmosphere: a hiking tour across the mystical landscape of this national park is an adventure → p. 60

⭐ **Greenway**
Romantic with a boathouse and overlooking the river: Agatha Christie's summerhouse on the River Dart is surrounded by a fabulous garden → p. 64

⭐ **Dartmouth Steam Railway**
Old steam engines cruise from Paignton to the small village of Kingswear → p. 65

⭐ **Exeter Cathedral**
An amazing architectural landmark: one of England's most beautiful cathedrals in the heart of Exeter → p. 67

⭐ **Barbican**
In the old harbour district of Plymouth you can immerse yourself in the past. Time seems to have stood still here – well, almost → p. 71

⭐ **Burgh Island**
The small tidal island with its steep coastline is home to the legendary Burgh Island Hotel → p. 73

## SIGHTSEEING

### DARTMOUTH CASTLE ☆

The imposing fortress is one of the most attractive of its kind and sits on the promontory on the Dart Estuary. At the highest point, there is a breathtaking view across the river. Dartmouth Castle once protected the vital waterway leading inland. *April–Oct daily, Nov–March Sat/Sun 10am–4pm | admission £6.60 | Castle Road | www.english-heritage.org.uk*

## FOOD & DRINK

### THE LAUGHING MONK ⓥ

Fine British food with locally sourced products. The restaurant is in a small former school. *Totnes Road | tel. 01803 77 06 39 | www.thelaughingmonkdevon.co.uk | Expensive*

## LOW BUDGET

● *Exeter Cathedral* has an admission fee, like many cathedrals. If you participate in the *Sunday Communion service (start 10am)*, you can enter free of charge and also experience a wonderful church service. Please respect that photographs are not allowed during the service.

Eating out in the evening can be expensive. However, some pubs have special discounts on specific days that often include a free drink with the meal – for example, *Union Rooms (19 Union Street | tel. 01752 25 45 20)* in Plymouth.

## WHERE TO STAY

### INSIDER TIP KINGSWEAR CASTLE

The old fort by the water's edge has been converted to a holiday home with two bedrooms and is available for four-day short breaks. *Castle Road | tel. 01628 82 59 25 | www.landmarktrust.org.uk | Moderate*

### ROYAL CASTLE HOTEL

Located on the quayside, this hotel is the perfect spot for exploring the town. Simple but stylish rooms. *24 rooms | 11 The Quay | tel. 01803 83 30 33 | www.royalcastle.co.uk | Moderate*

## INFORMATION

*Dartmouth Tourist Information | The Engine House | Mayor's Avenue | tel. 01803 83 42 24 | www.discoverdartmouth.com*

## WHERE TO GO

### GREENWAY ★ ☆ (125 E4) (𝄞 O8)

The picturesque house on the River Dart belonged to Agatha Christie for many years. She spent the summers here where she perfected her bestselling stories, although she didn't compose any here. However, Greenway features in her book "Dead Man's Folly".

The bright country house is still filled with all kinds of items that were kept here during Christie's time – including personal photos and her Order of the British Empire. You can stroll through the wonderful garden past a Victorian greenhouse and the Boathouse by the river. The National Trust also rents INSIDER TIP holiday cottages *(Moderate)* on the estate. *March–Oct daily 10.30am–5pm, Nov/Dec Sat/Sun (daily between Christmas and New Year) 11am–4pm | admission £11 | Greenway Road | Galmp-*

Dartmouth Steam Railway goes full steam ahead from Kingswear to Paignton!

ton | parking must be pre-booked by telephone | tel. 0844 3 35 12 87 (*) | www. nationaltrust.org.uk/greenway | 10 km/ 6.2 mi north

### KINGSWEAR (125 E5) (*N O9*)

The small town (pop. 1,200) on the river opposite Dartmouth has quaint and colourful cottages. This picturesque setting is a lovely place for a walk. The steam engines of the ★ ● ⚡ *Dartmouth Steam Railway (several times a week | return £16.75 | The Square | Kingswear | tel. 01803 55 58 72 | www.dartmouthrailriver. co.uk | 1 km/0.6 mi east)* travel from here to Paignton. *Ferries (Mon–Sat 7.30am– 11pm, Sun 9am–11pm | £1.50 per trip | www.dartmouthrailriver.co.uk)* connect Kingswear with Dartmouth about every 15 minutes during the day.

### SALCOMBE WITH START POINT LIGHTHOUSE
### (125 D–E6) (*N N10*)

Romantic Salcombe (pop. 2,000) on Kingsbridge Estuary offers plenty of scope for photos. The small, old houses are concentrated in the centre of town and there is a beach by the river. In the pink striped shop *Cranch (78 Fore Street)* you can enjoy a moment of nostalgia – since 1869, the store has sold brightly coloured sweets here. It is well worth visiting **INSIDER TIP** *Start Point Lighthouse (open on specific dates | admission £5 | www. startpointdevon.co.uk)*, which was built on a spectacular clifftop on the south coast. Enjoy the wonderful views over the river and stopover at the chic ⚡ *Salcombe Harbour Hotel & Spa (53 rooms | Cliff Road | tel. 01548 84 44 44 |*

A small town set in undulating countryside: picturesque Salcombe is situated on a river estuary

*www.salcombe-harbour-hotel.co.uk | Expensive). www.salcombeinformation.co. uk | 33 km/21 mi south-west*

# EXETER

### ⁘ MAP INSIDE BACK COVER
*(125 E–F1) (Ⓜ O5)* **Devon's capital city (pop. 125,000) was heavily bombed in the Blitz during the Second World War, but the character of the important trading centre was mainly preserved.**

At the heart of the city is the light sandstone St Peter Cathedral. On the main shopping area along the High Street you will notice various architectural styles dating back to Tudor times. A large part of the city wall dates to the period

of the Roman occupation (50–410 A.D.). Amidst the hustle and bustle the city appears to have more young people than are residents here: over 20,000 students attend the University of Exeter. There are free guided tours of the city every day at 11am and 2pm with the ● *Red Coat Guided Tours (Cathedral main entrance | tel. 01392 26 52 03 | www.exeter.gov.uk).*

> **Ⓒ WHERE TO START?**
> **Exeter Cathedral (U D2–3)** *(Ⓜ d2–3):* If you are coming by car, it's best to leave it in the carpark at John Lewis and stroll down the High Street to Queen Street. Turn left and the alley leads you directly to the cathedral.

## SIGHTSEEING

### EXETER CATHEDRAL ★
(U D2–3) (*m* d2–3)

You have to marvel at Exeter's St Peter Cathedral (built 1275–1369), which sits on the green at *Cathedral Yard,* and is obviously the most impressive building in the city centre. The west front of the sandstone building presents a wealth of stone statues from the bible and above it a wonderful traceried window. Inside you should look at the Gothic fan vaulted ceiling which is among the longest of its kind. There are free guided tours of the building several times a day. *Mon–Sat 9am–5pm, Sun 11.30am–5pm* | *admission £7.50* | *1 The Cloisters* | *www.exeter-cathedral.org.uk*

### ROYAL ALBERT MEMORIAL MUSEUM
(U C2) (*m* c2)

The extensive renovation of the neo-Gothic building is more than a local museum. You can visit the major exhibition on the history of Great Britain as well as the region around Exeter. The art collection also has an excellent reputation countrywide. *Tue–Sun 10am–5pm* | *free admission* | *Queen Street* | *www.rammuseum.org.uk*

### UNDERGROUND PASSAGES
(U D2) (*m* d2)

These Underground Passages record history: visitors can walk beneath the High Street through the old 14th century passages designed to carry water and enjoy a different view of Exeter. The passages are narrow, damp and dark, but you can also see the ruins of the old city gate. *June–Sept Mon–Sat 9.30am–5.30pm, Sun 10.30am–4pm, Oct–May Tue–Fri 10.30am–4.40pm, Sat 9.30am–5.30pm, Sun 11.30am–4pm* | *admission £6* | *2 Paris Street (entrance by Next)*

## FOOD & DRINK

### BOSTON TEA PARTY ⊛ (U C2) (*m* c2)

Coffee shop popular with students in the town centre that serves good coffee, fresh juices and a wide range of tasty dishes, everything is organic. *84 Queen Street* | *tel. 01392 20 11 81* | *www.bostonteaparty.co.uk* | *Budget*

### THE IMPERIAL (U B1) (*m* b1)

Inviting large pub in a former hotel high above St David's railway station. A wide menu choice until late in the evenings. In summer visitors can enjoy the pleasant INSIDER TIP▶ beer garden and licensed outdoor area. *New North Road* | *tel. 01392 43 40 50* | *Budget*

## SHOPPING

Exeter's town centre offers all kinds of shops from the *John Lewis Department Store* (U D2) (*m* d2) (*1 Sidwell Street*) to smaller shops at the opposite end of the pedestrian area.

## ENTERTAINMENT

Exeter's nightlife is all about students. Concerts and parties are held in *Lemon Grove* (0) (*m* 0) (*St. German's Road* | *tel. 01392 72 61 73* | *www.exeterguild.org/lemongrove)* and a popular place for cocktails is *Monkey Suit* (U E1) (*m* e1) (*161 Sidwell Street* | *www.themonkeysuit.co.uk).*

## WHERE TO STAY

### HOTEL DU VIN (U D3) (*m* d3)

A former Eye Infirmary was refurbished as a stylish boutique hotel with spa and fitness centre. *59 rooms* | *Magdalen Street* | *tel. 01392 28 10 00* | *www.hotelduvin.com/locations/exeter* | *Expensive*

**SOUTHGATE HOTEL** (U D3) (*d3*)
Stylish and comfortable four-star hotel in a central location with swimming pool and parking. *154 rooms | Southernhay East | tel. 01392 4128 12 | www.mercure. com | Expensive*

## INFORMATION

*Exeter Visitor Centre* (U D2) (*d2*) | *Dix's Field | tel. 01392 66 57 00 | www. heartofdevon.com/exeter*

## WHERE TO GO

### POWDERHAM CASTLE
(125 F2) (*O6*)
The home of the Earl of Devon still has the appearance of a medieval castle. Built between 1390 and 1420, much of the castle is preserved with numerous furniture items. Inside, you can still find secret doors. The castle grounds also offer an American Garden and knot garden. Don't miss the estate's ☻ INSIDER TIP *Farm Store (www.powderhamfarmshop.co.uk)*. You can find locally grown produce and for gardening enthusiasts there is a large selection of plants. *April–Oct Sun–Fri 11am–4.30pm | admission £12.95 | Kenton | www.powderham.co.uk | 13 km/ 8.1 mi south*

# EXMOUTH

(120 C6) (*P6*) **At a first glance, you might think that the town has seen better days. But many parts of Devon's oldest seaside resort have notably improved in recent years.**

The promenade is still influenced by Victorian houses and the 3 km/1.9 mi stretch of sandy beach. The buildings date from Exmouth's (pop. 33,000) heyday thanks to the railway link. The old port has been renovated with a mix of brightly coloured houses and the small boats in the marina offer a romantic setting on warm summer evenings. The *Jurassic Coast* begins at the rocky coastal feature at nearby Orcombe Point (see p. 71).

## SIGHTSEEING

### A LA RONDE
Who would have imagined building a 16-sided house? The two cousins Jane and Mary Parminter loved eccentric things, as you will notice from this curiously shaped building dating to the 18th century. They not only designed their house but also some furniture items. No less than 20 rooms are arranged around an octagonal centre. The house is still furnished exactly how it was left by both cousins. *Feb–Oct daily 11am–17pm | admission £8.90 | Summer Lane | www.nationaltrust.org. uk/a-la-ronde*

## FOOD & DRINK

### BUMBLE AND BEE ☻
Stylish small café offering a selection of tasty warm dishes. The chef only uses seasonal and locally sourced products. *Manor Gardens | Alexandra Terrace | tel. 07791 22 97 41 | www.bumbleandbee. co.uk | Moderate*

### RIVER EXE CAFÉ ☻
Probably the town's most unusual restaurant is on a barge that floats off shore in the Exe Estuary. Dishes include fresh seafood and vegetarian options, all prepared with locally sourced produce. *The Docks | accessed by water taxi (£5 return) from Point Bar Grill on the marina | tel. 07761 11 61 03 | www. riverexecafe.com | Expensive*

Thinking outside the box: the eccentric house A La Ronde in Exmouth

## LEISURE & SPORT

Exmouth is a ● centre for water sports enthusiasts and a wide range of activities are possible from surfing to canoeing and rowing. You can hire equipment at several points along the promenade such as *Exmouth Watersports (The Esplanade | tel. 01395 27 65 99 | www.ex mouthwatersports.co.uk)*.

## WHERE TO STAY

### THE DOLPHIN HOTEL

Family-run hotel in the city centre with small, but comfortable rooms. *26 rooms | 2 Morton Road | tel. 01395 26 38 32 | www.dolphinhotelexmouth. co.uk | Moderate*

## INFORMATION

*Exmouth Tourist Information Centre | 42 The Strand | tel. 01395 83 05 50 | www. exmouth-guide.co.uk*

## WHERE TO GO

### EAST DEVON AREA OF OUTSTANDING NATURAL BEAUTY ☆

(121 D–E 5) (*ØØ Q–R 5–6*)

The 100 mi² area near Seaton is known for its undulating grasslands and small woodlands. It is classified as one of Great Britain's *Areas of Outstanding Natural Beauty* and enjoys special protection. The area from Exmouth and Lyme Regis from the *Jurassic Coast* also stretches inland. It is ideal for hiking and the region can

In Plymouth's old harbour in the Barbican district, the past comes alive

beach, you can climb the wooden steps at *Jacob's Ladder* to *Connaught Gardens,* a pleasant garden on the sandstone clifftop. The ☆ INSIDERTIP *Clock Tower Café (Peak Hill Road | tel. 01395 51 53 19 | www.clocktowercafesidmouth.co.uk | Budget)* at the top of the hill not only offers panoramic sea views but provides a mouthwatering selection of cakes and light snacks. *www.visitsidmouth.co.uk | 18 km/11.2 mi north-east*

# PLYMOUTH

### MAP INSIDE BACK COVER
**(124 A–B5) (*M L9*) The old maritime town of Plymouth (pop. 260,000) in the far west of Devon has immense charm and its ports still radiate an atmosphere of openness towards the outside world.**

The rest of the town grew up in the 1950s — after heavy bombing during the Blitz in the Second World War. The town's architecture is functional rather than attractive. Sir Francis Drake, James Cook and Charles Darwin set out from Plymouth across the ocean and here the Royal Navy still maintains the largest military port in Western Europe. The pedestrian area is a pleasant destination for a shopping trip.

also be explored on an old railway track: INSIDERTIP *Seaton Tramway (April–Oct daily 10am–4pm, scheduled dates in winter | £10 | Riverside Depot | Harbour Road | Seaton | tel. 01297 2 03 75 | www.tram.co.uk)* which runs from the coast about 5 km/3.1 mi to Colyton. *www.eastdevonaonb.org.uk*

### SIDMOUTH (121 D5) (*M Q6*)
One of the jewels on the *Jurassic Coast is* Sidmouth (pop. 13,000) nestled among the red sandstone cliffs and protected by grassy headlands. From the main

> **CITY** **WHERE TO START?**
> **Barbican district (U D–E 5–6)** **(*M d–e 5–6*):** It's best to park at one of the car parks on Lambhay Hill, then you can relax and explore the old harbour with its narrow streets. From here you can stroll to limestone cliff ☆ The Hoe to enjoy a fantastic panoramic view of the harbour.

## SIGHTSEEING

### BARBICAN ★
(U D–E 5–6) (𝄞 d–e 5–6)

The old harbour is Plymouth's jewel. The small houses along the quayside almost make you step back in time. Not much seems to have changed down the centuries, only the boats in the harbour look modern. *Black Friars Distillery (Mon–Sat 10am–5pm, Sun 10am–4pm | Tour £7 | 60 Southside Street | tel. 01752 66 52 92 | www.plymouthgin.com)* has produced Plymouth Gin here since 1783.

### THE HOE ⛱
(U C–D 5–6) (𝄞 c–d 5–6)

The limestone cliff in the centre is one of Plymouth's most impressive places. There is a wonderful view of the harbour and sea from the clifftop. The red and white lighthouse *Smeaton's Tower (daily 10am–5pm | admission £4 | Hoe Road)* has a majestic clifftop position like a city landmark. In 1588, Sir Francis Drake is said to have played a game of bowls on The Hoe before he put to sea to defeat the Spanish Armada. A statue on the green immortalises the mariner.

### NATIONAL MARINE AQUARIUM ●
(U E5) (𝄞 e5)

Great Britain's biggest aquarium also has the deepest tank in the country. It contains not only fish from the Atlantic and the surrounding area but also fish in a special tropical tank. *Daily 10am–5pm | admission £15.95 | Rope Walk | Coxside | www.national-aquarium.co.uk*

### ROYAL WILLIAM YARD (0) (𝄞 0)

The largest military area in west Plymouth was once a victualling depot for the Royal Navy. Behind the majestic entrance gate is an entire district with renovated warehouses, businesses and retailers. Former abattoirs and bakeries now house cafés and restaurants that offer gastro food and trendy drinks and are mainly situated on the quayside. A **INSIDER TIP** ▶ *Ferry service (daily 10am–5pm, in summer until 6pm | per trip £3 | www.silverlinecruises.co.uk)* connects Royal William Yard with the Barbican district – ferries depart every hour.

# ON THE TRAIL OF THE DINOSAURS

Scientists can read the rocky cliffs along the *Jurassic Coast* like a book. For everyone else this 150 km/93 mi stretch of coastline offers primarily one thing: stunning scenery with sensational rocky cliffs. From Orcombe Point near Exmouth to Old Harry Rocks in Dorset you will find many different attractions of this Unesco World Heritage Site, including the unusual red sandstone clifftops in East Devon. Near Beer, you can explore the sand limestone caves. The Jurassic Coast ac-quired its name due to the many fossils found here dating from the Jurassic period. Some of these are displayed at the ● *Sidmouth Museum (April–Oct Mon 1pm–4pm, Tue–Sat 10am–4pm | free admission | Hope Cottage | Church Street | Sidmouth | www.devonmuseums. net)*. Guided fossil tours can be booked via the *Charmouth Heritage Coast Centre (specified dates | booking required | £8 | Lower Sea Lane | Charmouth | tel. 01297 56 07 72 | www.charmouth.org/ chcc)*.

**SALTRAM** (0) *(𝄢 0)*

An impressive country house in a wonderful parkland estate on the River Plym. You can tour the luxuriously furnished rooms with Chinese wallpaper and many historic and valuable paintings. "Sense and Sensibility" based on the novel by Jane Austen was filmed here in 1995. *Park daily 10am–4pm, house 11am–3.30pm | admission £11 | Plympton | www.nationaltrust.org.uk/saltram*

## FOOD & DRINK

**BISTROT PIERRE** (0) *(𝄢 0)*

This French-style restaurant serves an excellent choice of Anglo-French cuisine. Healthy dishes feature plenty of fish, vegetables and meat options. *New Cooperage | Royal William Yard | tel. 01752 26 23 18 | short.travel/cod9 | Expensive*

**CROWN AND ANCHOR** (U E5) *(𝄢 e5)*

Pub food from *fish & chips* to steak: this pub in the historic harbour district is always busy. Hearty food and reasonable prices. *10 The Barbican | tel. 01752 22 45 72 | Budget*

## LEISURE & SPORT

**TINSIDE LIDO** ⚹ (U C6) *(𝄢 c6)*

The Tinside Lido, built in 1935 in Art Deco style, is one of the most attractive open-air pools in the country and offers spectacular views over the sea and town. *June–Sept. Mon–Fri noon–6pm, Sat/Sun 10am–6pm | admission £4.75 | Hoe Road*

## ENTERTAINMENT

*Barbican Bluesbar* (U D5) *(𝄢 d5) (8 The Parade | tel. 01752 25 73 45 | www.bluesbarandgrill.co.uk)* is a popular spot for good live music (Blues, Jazz). In *Annabel's Cabaret* (U E5) *(𝄢 e5) (88 Vauxhall Street | tel. 01752 26 05 55)* there is a buzzing party scene and live music (Rock).

## WHERE TO STAY

**BORINGDON HALL** (0) *(𝄢 0)*

The Elizabethan manor house has been renovated and became an exclusive luxury hotel, which offers a spa area, a large swimming pool and fine restaurant. *41 rooms | Colebrook | Plympton | tel. 01752 34 44 55 | www.boringdonhall.co.uk | Expensive*

**SEA BREEZES** (U B6) *(𝄢 b6)*

A small guesthouse with pleasant and comfortable rooms, some with sea views. *8 rooms | 28 Grand Parade | West Hoe | tel. 01752 667205 | www.plymouth-bedandbreakfast.co.uk | Budget*

## INFORMATION

*Tourist Information Centre* (U E5) *(𝄢 e5) | Plymouth Mayflower 3–5 | The Barbican | tel. 01752 30 63 30 | www.visitplymouth.co.uk*

## WHERE TO GO

**BUCKLAND ABBEY** (124 A3) *(𝄢 L8)*

The medieval abbey with its imposing nave is the perfect backdrop for a religious crime thriller, but down the centuries this was a private residence. Buckland Abbey was built in 1278 as a Cistercian abbey and, like all England's monasteries, it was closed during the monarch's dissolution of the monasteries. In 1541, Sir Richard Grenville converted the abbey to a private residence and later sold it to the famous circumnavigator Sir Francis Drake. *Feb–Oct daily*

Small Burgh Island is a tidal island – at low tide, you can walk over to it

*11am–5pm, Nov Sat/Sun 11am–4pm, Dec daily 11am–4pm | Yelverton | www.nationaltrust.org.uk/buckland-abbey | admission £11 | 15 km/9.3 mi north*

**BURGH ISLAND ★ ● ☀**
(124 C6) (*🕮 M9*)
Agatha Christie is said to have written "Evil under the Sun" in the Burgh Island Hotel. But you don't need to stay at the hotel – the rugged, small tidal island is well worth a visit. At low tide, it takes only a few minutes to walk from *Bigbury Bay,* while at high tide you take a *Sea Tractor (£2, free for hotel guests).* The island has rocky cliffs and the ruins of a small medieval chapel as well as the quaint *Pilchard Inn* with centuries of history. Of course, you can also stopover at *Burgh Island Hotel (25 rooms | Burgh Island | Bigbury-on-Sea | tel. 01548 810514 | www.burghisland.com | Expensive).* 31 km/19.3 mi east

# TORQUAY

(125 E–F 3–4) (*🕮 O7–8*) **Torquay (pop. 65,000), once a magnificent seaside resort, may look a little run down but tourists still arrive by the bus load.**
The town is often regarded as a town for retirees and yet it is a popular tourist destination thanks to the picturesque bay and geological conditions – the locals say that Torquay, like Rome, is built on seven hills. In fact, there are almost 40 hills. The beaches are fabulous and the pedestrian zone is also a busy hub in south Devon. The "Queen of Crime",

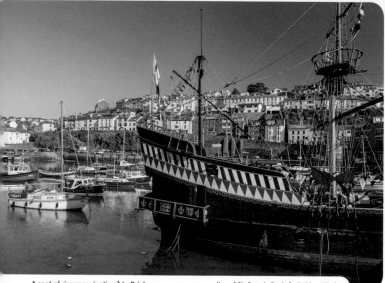

A spot of circumnavigation? In Brixham, you can see a replica of Sir Francis Drake's *Golden Hind*

Agatha Christie, was born here in 1890. Every September a literature festival is held in her honour.

## SIGHTSEEING

### KENTS CAVERN ●

The oldest known occupied caves in Great Britain are a fantastic contrast to Torquay's summer beach life. People once lived here during the Stone Age – scientists have discovered objects dating back more than 450,000 years. An upper jaw bone discovered in Kents Cavern is believed to be more than 40,000 years old, making it the oldest remains of modern man in Europe. *Daily 10am–5pm | admission £10 | 91 Ilsham Road | www.kents-cavern.co.uk*

### TORRE ABBEY

This wonderful mixture of medieval abbey and Georgian country manor is home to a fascinating museum about the history of the region. Torre Abbey was founded in 1196 as a monastery and during the 15th century developed into one of the wealthiest of its kind throughout England – until Henry VIII ordered its dissolution like all English monasteries. The INSIDER TIP garden is interesting: this special area exclusively contains plants that were used as poisons in Agatha Christie's novels. *June–Sept daily, otherwise Wed–Sun 10am–5pm | admission £8, | The Kings Drive | www.torre-abbey. org.uk*

## FOOD & DRINK

### THE LONDON INN

The spacious pub offers a generous selection of beer to sample while watching a live match. You can try the INSIDER TIP local beer served draught at the same time. *16 Strand | tel. 01803 38 00 03 | Budget*

## NUMBER 7 ⊙

Excellent fish restaurant on the harbourside where guests choose the fresh fish before it is prepared. The products are locally sourced from the region. *7 Beacon Hill | tel. 01803 29 50 55 | www.no7-fish.com | Expensive*

## SHOPPING

*Fleet Street* with its shopping centre *Fleet Walk* is the town's main shopping area. Many chains have opened branches of their stores here. However, you will not find any large department stores, apart from a modest *Debenhams* on the harbourside. *Cockington Court* slightly outside town has a pleasant craft centre.

## BEACHES

There are about a dozen beaches along the bay of Torbay, some of them are sandy and others shingle beaches. All are well maintained. The best beaches are at *Broadsands* and *Paignton*.

## WHERE TO STAY

### THE CLEVELAND

Small Bed & Breakfast slightly uphill from the town centre. Comfortable and quiet. *7 rooms | 7 Cleveland Road | tel. 01803 29 75 22 | www.clevelandbandbtorquay. co.uk | Budget*

### THE IMPERIAL HOTEL ✲

Elegant 19th-century hotel. A fabulous location for INSIDER TIP *afternoon tea* with views overlooking the harbour. *152 rooms | Park Hill Road | tel. 01803 29 43 01 | www.theimperialtorquay.co. uk | Expensive*

## INFORMATION

*English Riviera Visitor Information Centre | 5 Vaughan Parade | tel. 01803 21 12 11 | www.englishriviera.co.uk*

## WHERE TO GO

**BRIXHAM** (125 E–F4) *(⌀ O8)*
The picturesque town (pop. 16,000) in Torbay's south district has survived on its fishing industry for almost 1,000 years. It has colourful houses and small boats. The *Fish Market (tours on fixed dates, Wednesday mornings | booking at bfmt2014@gmail.com)* is still an important port for local fishing boats. In the harbour, there are excellent restaurants like the modern ✲ *Rockfish (The Harbour | tel. 01803 85 08 72 | www.therockfish. co.uk | Moderate)* with great views over the bay. There is also a replica of Francis Drake's flagship, the *Golden Hind II (March–Oct daily 10am–4pm | admission from £7 | The Quay). 13 km/8.1 mi south*

**PAIGNTON** (125 E4) *(⌀ O8)*
The little sister to Torquay has an unfortunate reputation as a cheap seaside resort. But Paignton (pop. 50,000) has several attractions like *Oldway Mansion (daily 9.30am–4.30pm | free admission | Torquay Road)*. The American sewing machine producer Isaac Merritt Singer had this country house with vast park estate built at the end of the 19th century. On the upper floor, there is a hall of mirrors in the style of the Palace of Versailles. *Dartmouth Steam Railway (see p. 65)* cruises from Paignton's *Queens Park Station* to Dartmouth (10.8 km/ 6.7 mi). Situated on the promenade is the hotel *The Palace (55 rooms | Esplanade Road | tel. 01803 55 51 21 | www.palacepaignton.com | Expensive). 6 km/3.7 mi south*

# NORTH DEVON

**Something for connoisseurs: North Devon, unlike the south, has fewer internationally renowned locations but that also defines its charm.**

You can see the dramatic rocky clifftops, attractive beaches and endless undulating countryside as well as misty fields inland. Rather like the rest of Devon, you might say? Well, almost. The northern part is more rugged and the countryside is often more isolated than in other areas of the county. While Exmoor only covers part of Devon, it is undoubtedly one of England's most beautiful spots – not only because of the ubiquitous Exmoor ponies and numerous sheep. You can discover plenty of small villages without the monotonous retail chains, and where owner-run shops and craftsmen keep up some old English traditions. You can relax and unwind along the coast with views overlooking the Bristol Channel.

# BARNSTAPLE

**(119 D2–3) (🗺 L2) The old market town of Barnstaple (pop. 24,000) is the main town in North Devon.**

The hustle and bustle of the town centre is noticeable at midday when people from around the area arrive to do their shopping. There are numerous grocery stores around the old *Pannier Market*, most of them are specialist shops like delicatessens and takeaway coffee shops.

Rocky coasts and undulating countryside: North Devon still has many unspoilt areas like a hundred years ago

## SIGHTSEEING

### MUSEUM OF BARNSTAPLE AND NORTH DEVON

The perfect introduction to the history of North Devon. The museum presents displays about the development of Barnstaple and the local region. In front of the museum is the historic *Albert Clock,* which commemorates Queen Victoria's Prince Consort and husband, Albert of Saxe-Coburg and Gotha. *March–Oct Mon–Sat 10am–5pm,* *Nov–Feb 10am–4pm | free admission | The Square | www.barnstaplemuseum. org.uk*

### PANNIER MARKET

Barnstaple's market hall was a model for many others in Devon. Since the mid-19th century, market traders have offered their merchandise here. The Pannier Market has more or less become a permanent flea market. *Mon–* *Sat 9am–3pm | Butchers Row | www. barnstaple.co.uk/pannier-market/*

Hiking? Or preferably cycling? On the Tarka Trail you can do both!

## FOOD & DRINK

### INSIDERTIP ALEXANDER'S SANDWICH BAR

Known locally as the best sandwich shop in town, the freshly prepared doorsteps surpass any pre-packaged version. *31 C Boutport Street | tel. 01271 37 37 35 | Budget*

### ALFIE BROWN'S

This comfortable pub serves good hearty English cuisine. *54 Boutport Street | tel. 01271 34 44 77 | www.alfiebrowns.co.uk | Moderate*

## WHERE TO STAY

### THE IMPERIAL HOTEL

Classical English hotel – more old style comfort than contemporary. *63 rooms | Taw Vale | tel. 01271 34 58 61 | www.brend-imperial.co.uk | Moderate*

### TARKA BED AND BREAKFAST

Simple guesthouse outside Barnstaple in a beautiful countryside setting. *3 rooms | 25 Chilpark | Fremington | tel. 01271 32 35 26 | Budget*

## INFORMATION

*Tourist Information Centre | The Square | tel. 01271 37 50 00 | www.barnstaple.co.uk*

## WHERE TO GO

### TARKA TRAIL ☼
### (119 D–F 1–3) (𝄞 L–M 1–2)

The Tarka Trail, about 290 km/180 mi, is traffic-free and set in beautiful countryside. You can explore the trail on foot or by bicycle. From Barnstaple it follows a circular route via Braunton, Ilfracombe and Lynton and back. About 50 km/31.1 mi of the route continues along a reused railway track. The trail is named after Tarka the Otter, a story by Henry Williamson. You can hire bicycles for a tour from *Tarka Bikes (The Railway Station | Barnstaple | tel. 01271 32 42 02 | www.tarkabikes.co.uk).*

### WESTWARD HO! (118 C3) (𝄞 K3)

This seaside resort (pop. 2,000) is mainly famous for its spelling: it is the only place in Europe officially ending with an exclamation mark. The name is based on the novel by Charles Kingsley who persuaded investors to build the town. Westward Ho! is popular because of its extensive beach. Nearby is *Appledore*, a romantic fishing village that still thrives thanks to its shipyard. *17 km/10.6 mi west*

# EXMOOR

**(119 E–F 1–3) (*M–O 1–2*) This national park with natural valleys and hidden villages offers open moorlands leading to steep rocky coasts.**

The moors seem to stretch endlessly with mist-filled valleys – Exmoor has almost ghostly but attractive scenery. Near the source of the River Exe is one Great Britain's most spectacular moorlands. The area is well known for the oldest breed of ponies on the British Isles: the Exmoor Pony. It also has plenty of small bilberry bushes growing on the open moorland. Only part of Exmoor is in Devon – the rest is in Somerset.

## SIGHTSEEING

### DUNSTER CASTLE

A picture book castle: Dunster Castle sits above the medieval town of *Dunster* (pop. 800) with its towers and battlements. Inside, the Victorian furnishings make it obvious that the building is more contemporary than you think. The castle dates to the 19th century. The parkland setting is wonderful and a narrow footpath leads to a romantic Watermill Tearoom and café. *Castle March–Oct daily 11am–5pm, Dec Sat/Sun 11am–3pm, Park March–Oct daily 10am–5pm, Nov–Feb 11am–4pm | admission £11, park only £8 | www.nationaltrust.org.uk/dunster-castle*

### LYNTON/LYNMOUTH ★

Two towns for the price of two: while Lynton proudly sits on the clifftops of Exmoor, down below Lynmouth developed into a sleepy seaside village. The two places are linked by the water-powered funicular *Cliff Railway (daily 10am–5pm, in summer until 9pm | single £2.80, return £3.80 | The Esplanade Lynmouth | tel. 01598 75 39 08 | www.cliffrailwaylynton.co.uk)* which takes visitors back centuries: the tank of a carriage is filled with water until it is heavy enough to descend into the valley. The same principle has been in operation since 1890. There is a spectacular view at the top from the ✹ INSIDER TIP *Cliff Top Café (Lee Road | tel. 01598 75 33 66).*

## MARCO POLO HIGHLIGHTS

★ **Lynton/Lynmouth**
The lovely two small towns are connected via an old water-powered funicular
→ p. 79

★ **Valley of the Rocks**
Impressive rocky clifftops form this small valley in Exmoor → p. 80

★ **Clovelly**
A small fishing village in a romantic setting – and traffic-free → p. 83

★ **Verity**
Damien Hirst's bronze statue on the pier at Ilfracombe caused a furore when it was unveiled
→ p. 84

★ **Lundy Island**
The island on an outcrop off North Devon is a paradise for nature fans → p. 85

## PORLOCK

This enchanted village (pop. 1,400) in the north of Exmoor is an English picture book village. The high street winds its way through Porlock and is also one of the central arteries crossing Exmoor from west to east. The aroma of coffee is in the air because INSIDER TIP *DJ Miles (The Vale Yard | High Street)*, a fine coffee roastery, was established here and produces excellent blends. *Porlock Weir,* which is inland from the village, is also attractive.

## VALLEY OF THE ROCKS ★ ☼

Don't be alarmed if a goat crosses your path here. On the coast between Lynton and Porlock, nature has created a unique scenic location with impressive, rocky stone hills partly overgrown with grass. The *feral goats* live here and obviously enjoy the fabulous views. You should join them!

## LOW BUDGET

Spend and save: there are numerous outlet malls in the area offering designer goods at discount prices. One of the outlet villages, near Bideford, has 35 shops and is known as ● *Atlantic Village (Clovelly Road | Bideford | www.atlanticvillage.co.uk).*

Train travel can be expensive, but you can easily cut costs: if you travel off-peak, tickets are cheaper than during peak times. You can also save money by booking in advance – selecting your train time makes the price even more reasonable. You can get all the details at *www.thetrainline.com* (also available as a smartphone app).

### FOOD & DRINK

#### THE CASTLE ●

Pleasant pub in the centre of Porlock, hearty English cuisine and guest rooms. *High Street | Porlock | tel. 01643 86 25 04 | www.thecastleporlock.co.uk | Moderate*

#### THE RISING SUN ◉

The rustic exterior is deceptive: this pub serves fine cuisine with freshly caught fish and other local products. *Lynmouth Street | Harbourside | Lynmouth | tel. 01598 75 32 23 | Expensive*

### WHERE TO STAY

#### MILLERS AT THE ANCHOR

Sleepy boutique hotel with open fire in Porlock Weir by the harbourside. *14 rooms | Porlock Weir | tel. 01643 86 27 53 | www.millersuk.com/anchor | Expensive*

### INFORMATION

*Lynmouth National Park Centre | The Pavilion | The Esplanade | Lynmouth | tel. 01598 75 25 09 | www.visit-exmoor.co.uk*

### WHERE TO GO

#### KNIGHTSHAYES (120 C3) (*Ø O4*)

A picturesque Victorian country house: Knightshayes looks like a majestic monastery but it was always "only" a private home. The rooms are mainly dark with eccentric Gothic revival decor. The house is surrounded by one of Devon's most attractive gardens. *March–Oct daily 10am–5pm, Nov–Feb 10am–4pm| admission £11 | Bolham | Tiverton | www.nationaltrust.org.uk/knightshayes*

Relaxing starting point for rambling tours across North Devon: Great Torrington

# GREAT TORRINGTON

**(119 D4)** *(ⓜ K3)* **Great Torrington (pop. 6,000) seems rather inconspicuous, but the small town offers more than you may think at a first glance.**

The town centre of Great Torrington has many medieval buildings. A quick tour of one of the side streets or the car park at the *Pannier Market* will quickly lead you to nature, since Great Torrington is surrounded by one of North Devon's most attractive countryside settings.

**PANNIER MARKET**

The small market hall has different offers every day and was formerly the trading hub of Great Torrington. The area in front of the town hall is now used as a place for market stalls. *Tue and Thu–Sat 9am–3pm | South Street*

**ROSEMOOR**

It's all in the name: about 2,000 roses and 200 different varieties grow in this garden outside Great Torrington. The garden is also a parkland. At Christmas, at twilight you can enjoy the

Cobblestone streets and small houses along the rocky coastline – Clovelly is amazingly picturesque

**INSIDER TIP** 'Glow' colourful illuminations. *April–Sept daily 10am–6pm, Oct–March 10am–5pm | admission £11 | A3124 | www. rhs.org.uk/gardens/rosemoor*

## FOOD & DRINK

### THE TORRIDGE INN
An unusual combination: Thai food is prepared in this rustic pub. *136 Mill Street | Taddiport | tel. 01805 62 50 42 | Moderate*

## WHERE TO STAY

### EASTMOND HOUSE
A simple Bed & Breakfast, no frills, but in a central location. *4 rooms | 4 Potacre Street | tel. 01805 62 34 11 | www.east mondhouse.co.uk | Budget*

## INFORMATION

*Tourist Information Centre | Castle Hill | tel. 01805 62 61 40 | www.great-torring ton.com*

## WHERE TO GO

### BIDEFORD
**(118 C3) (ⓜ K3)**
Bideford (pop. 17,000) is well known for its lovely old round-arched *Long Bridge* over the River Torridge. Measuring 200 m/660 ft in length, it is one of the longest bridges of its kind in England. Bideford also has a typical *Market Hall* with a weekly market on Tuesdays and Saturdays. Otherwise, the shops are mainly galleries and souvenir stores. Near the bridge, you will find *The*

Royal Hotel (32 rooms | Barnstaple Street | tel. 01237 47 20 05 | www.royalbideford. co.uk | Moderate). 12 km/7.5 mi north

## CLOVELLY ★ ☼ (118 B3) (⌀ J3)

There is a traffic ban here, and even pedestrians have to pay to enter this privately-owned village (pop. 400). But this makes it one of North Devon's most attractive destinations. Small cottages line the steep road downhill to the harbour; the cobblestones are made of local stone. This is a picture postcard setting and the harbour is romantic. The writer Charles Kingsley was born here. He immortalised Clovelly in his book "Westward Ho!" in which the character Salvation Yeo was born in what is currently the *Red Lion Hotel* (11 rooms | The Quay | tel. 01237 43 12 37 | *Moderate*). Daily 9am–6pm | admission £7.25 | www.clovelly.co.uk | 30 km/18.6 mi west

## HARTLAND COAST ☼
(118 A3) (⌀ H3)

The *Hartland Point Lighthouse* marks the area where the Bristol Channel flows into the Atlantic. The weather at the top is often bitter, windy and it is lonely, although this makes this hiking region in North Devon so magical. *Hartland Quay* was once a busy port that was gradually eroded due to the severe storms. Parts of the old quay wall are still visible at low tide. The relatively simple ☼ |INSIDER TIP| *Hartland Quay Hotel* (17 rooms | Hartland | Bideford | tel. 01237 44 12 18 | www.hartlandquayhotel.co.uk | *Moderate*) not only offers fabulous views, but also a small museum about the region's history. *Hartland Abbey,* a former abbey, is now a country house with lovely gardens (April–Sept Sun–Thu 11am–5pm, house 2pm–5pm | admission £12 | Hartland). 30 km/18.6 mi west

# ILFRACOMBE

(119 D1) (⌀ L1) **In a secluded spot, in the 19th century the town (pop. 12,000) tried to achieve a balance between the harbour and seaside resort.**

Today, the centre still showcases Victorian architecture, even if the paint is peeling off here and there. While no longer

# ON THE SMUGGLERS' ROUTE

Hiking trails galore – in Devon and Cornwall there are many unspoiled routes in secluded spots. The ★ ● ☼ South West Coast Path (www.southwest coastpath.org.uk) is pure enjoyment for nature lovers. The trail continues for 1014 km/630 mi along the coasts of both counties and beyond. The path begins at Minehead in Somerset on the edge of Exmoor and ends in Dorset, near Poole Harbour, Devon's neighbouring county. The best features are the perfect sea views from almost every point, the clifftops, secluded cabins and small villages. The path follows the entire coastline – originally, it was not a hiking route but was used by coastguards to stop smugglers moving quickly from one location to another. However, there is no need to walk the entire 1,014 km/630 mi trail, as a single section is an adventure! Simply follow the symbols along the route – a white acorn on a brown background.

a popular bathing resort, the town retains its maritime flair that is unrivalled in this area.

Ilfracombe has for a long while survived as a sleepy town with small boats in the harbour and the unmistakable feeling that here everyone has all the time in the world.

## SIGHTSEEING

### LANDMARK THEATRE

It is already eye catching from the promenade: two large cylinders seem to be propped on top of the flat building. Some people consider its appearance like a nuclear power plant. In Ilfracombe the locals refer to the controversial building as "Madonna's bra" because it looks like one of the bustiers that the pop diva once wore on stage. In 2017, the theatre went bankrupt and its performances are currently cancelled and the box office is closed. *Wilder Road*

### ST NICHOLAS CHAPEL ☆

The small chapel on the green at Lantern Hill by the harbourside was for centuries a destination for pilgrims. In the medieval period, it was used as a lighthouse. The steep uphill path is well worth the climb: you have a fabulous view of the village from here. *May–Sept daily 10am–6pm, April and Oct 10am–4pm | free admission | Lantern Hill*

### VERITY ★

In an atmospheric town like Ilfracombe you don't exactly expect top-class art – so, Damien Hirst's bronze statue "Verity" gets even more attention. It has stood on the pier at the entrance to the harbour since 2012. The statue is 20 m/65.6 ft tall and controversial: the sculpture shows a pregnant woman with raised sword and open womb revealing the foetus and organs inside. The statue caused a furore in the literary press. The town was unaccustomed to so much attention. The critics meanwhile accept that the scandalous lady enhances the location. Hirst has opened the small gallery *Other Criteria (10 The Quay | tel. 01271 86 70 57 | www.damienhirst.com)* in the town. *Harbour Front*

## FOOD & DRINK

### THE MANOR HOUSE CAFÉ ☺

Small café in the town centre with excellent warm dishes and a generous English breakfast. All the produce is locally sourced. *70 High Street | tel. 012 71 86 48 65 | www.themanorhousecafe. co.uk | Budget*

### THE QUAY ☺

Fine British cuisine with locally sourced products, inspired by the artist Damien Hirst. *11 The Quay | tel. 01271 86 80 90 | www.11thequay.co.uk | Expensive*

## WHERE TO STAY

### THE CARLTON HOTEL

A recently renovated, traditional hotel near the beach. *18 rooms | Runnacleave Road | tel. 01271 86 24 46 | www.ilfracom becarlton.co.uk | Moderate*

### WENTWORTH HOUSE

Small Bed & Breakfast in a Victorian building in the centre of Ilfracombe. *6 rooms | 2 Belmont Road | tel. 01271 86 30 48 | www.hotelilfracombe.co.uk | Budget*

## INFORMATION

*Tourist Information Centre | Landmark Theatre | Wilder Road | tel. 01271 86 30 01 | www.visitilfracombe.co.uk*

A secluded spot: on Lundy Island the black-backed gull feels at home

## WHERE TO GO

**ARLINGTON COURT** (119 E2) (*🕮 L2*)

The Regency country house looks as though it was recently vacated. Flowers bloom by the entrance, while inside there is an exhibition about everyday life in the 19th century. In the adjoining barn the *National Carriage Museum* presents about 40 horse-drawn vehicles from different eras. The garden is spectacular. *March–Oct daily 11am–5pm, Nov/Dec and Feb Sat/Sun 11am–4pm | admission £11 | Arlington | short.travel/cod5 | 20 km/12.4 mi north-west*

**LUNDY ISLAND ★** 

(118 A1–2) (*🕮 G1*)

This is the perfect spot for guaranteed relaxation: Lundy Island is a small island in the Bristol Channel. It is not always accessible, even in the summer, and takes two hours to reach on a return boat trip. On this rugged stretch of England there are impressive rocky outcrops and natural countryside – apart from a few houses, a lighthouse and the medieval small *Marisco Castle* there are mainly lambs, puffins and tremendous sea views from almost every point on the island. The Landmark Trust has converted many beautiful old buildings into overnight accommodation, so you can stopover surrounded by walls made from centuries-old sandstone. On specified dates there are INSIDER TIP day trips with the *MS Oldenburg (April–Oct approx. every other day | day trip £38, return £67)*, depending on tides from Bideford or Ilfracombe. In winter, on specific dates there is a *Helicopter (from Hartland Point | £119 return). Lundy Shore Office | The Quay | Bideford | tel. 01271 86 36 36 | www.lundyisland.co.uk | 25 km/15.5 mi west*

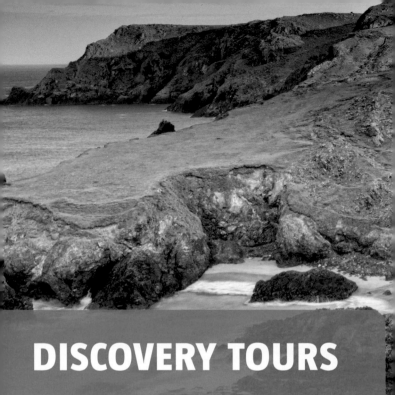

# DISCOVERY TOURS

## DEVON AND CORNWALL AT A GLANCE

**START:** ❶ Exeter
**END:** ❶ Exeter

**Distance:**
🚗 940 km/584 mi

**14 days**
Driving time
(without stops)
approx. 18 hours

**COSTS:** £1,300 to £2,200/person (depending on hotel category) for stopover in double room, food, admissions, petrol
**WHAT TO PACK:** hiking shoes, rain gear, sun protection in summer, warm clothes (even in summer), swimming kit

**IMPORTANT TIPS:** ⓯ **Isles of Scilly:** *Scillonian III* (only March–Nov | tel. 01736 33 42 20 | *www.islesofscilly-travel.co.uk*): check the timetable! ㉓ **Clovelly:** Please phone ahead for making pottery at **Clovelly Pottery**.

Would you like to explore the places that are unique to this region? Then the Discovery Tours are just the thing for you – they include terrific tips for stops worth making, breathtaking places to visit, selected restaurants and fun activities. It's even easier with the Touring App: download the tour with map and route to your smartphone using the QR Code on pages 2/3 or from the website address in the footer below – and you'll never get lost again, even when you're offline.

TOURING APP

→ p. 2/3

This circular tour takes you through Devon and Cornwall and back – past the quaintest harbours, coastlines and towns. If you prefer a more relaxed pace, simply stay for an extra day or two along the route.

You can start by walking around Devon's capital city **①** **Exeter** → p. 66. Start at the **Cathedral** and the remains of the **Roman City Wall** behind the church. Then, you can walk into the former chapel: INSIDER TIP **George's Meeting House** (*38 South Street | tel. 01392 45 42 50 | Budget*). The **Hôtel du Vin** in a wonderful old building is a

**DAY 1**
**①** Exeter

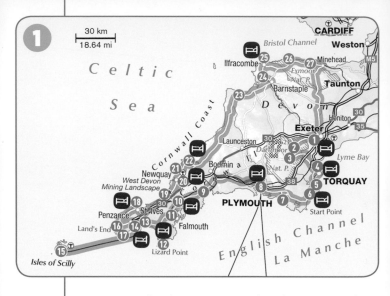

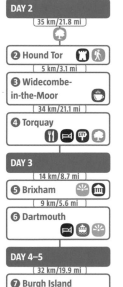

**DAY 2**

35 km/21.8 mi

**2 Hound Tor** 🏛️ 🚶

5 km/3.1 mi

**3 Widecombe-in-the-Moor** ☕

34 km/21.1 mi

**4 Torquay** 🍴 🛏️ 🍺 🌳

**DAY 3**

14 km/8.7 mi

**5 Brixham** 🏖️ 🏛️

9 km/5.6 mi

**6 Dartmouth** 🛏️ ⛴️ 🏖️

**DAY 4–5**

32 km/19.9 mi

**7 Burgh Island** 🚶 🌳 🏖️ 🍸

perfect place to stopover – and to enjoy some pampering in the hotel's **REN Spa**.

**Via the B3212** you arrive on picturesque Dartmoor. **About 1 km/0.6 mi after Bovey Castle on the left you arrive at 2 Hound Tor → p. 61**. Take the opportunity to explore the impressive granite rocks before you enjoy a *cream tea* at **3 Widecombe-in-the-Moor → p. 62** in the **Café on the Green**. In the evening head **onto the B3357, the A38 and A382 and continue to 4 Torquay → p. 73**, where you can stay overnight. Enjoy dinner with fresh fish at **Number 7** on the harbourside.

In the morning, you can explore Torquay's **town centre** and breathe in the sea air on the **beach**. Then continue driving **on Torbay Road and the A379 to 5 Brixham → p. 75** which is famous for its fishing boats. Don't miss: the view from the **harbour** and the **replica of the ship** the *Golden Hind*. Carry on **along Bolton Street and Drew Street to the A379 to 6 Dartmouth → p. 63** where you can stay overnight.

In Dartmouth, enjoy the fabulous view of the River Dart – ideally, on a **boat trip** from the harbour. Head **onto the A379 to 7 Burgh Island → p. 73 (detour at Bigbury onto** the B3392) which you can walk across to at low tide. Marvel at the rocky coastline on such a tiny island! On the way back, stop for a refreshing drink at the old pub, the **Pilchard Inn**. **Return via Bigbury and the A379 to ⑧ Plymouth → p. 70** where you stop over for two nights. The day begins with a walk on **The Hoe**. You can enjoy a fabulous panoramic view from the large park, especially from the lighthouse **Smeaton's Tower**. In the **Barbican** district, you can visit **Black Friars Distillery**, where Plymouth Gin is produced. Take the ferry to **Royal William Yard**, a former military shipyard – perfect for dinner and a pint.

Pack your suitcases and head for **Cornwall on the Devon Express Way (A38, A390):** at the ⑨ **Eden Project → p. 44** you can explore the world's climate zones at over 30° C/ 86° F and tropical humidity. In ⑩ **Truro → p. 46 (via A390)** you can explore Cornwall's capital city. You can plan an overnight stop here. The **pedestrian zone** is attractive for window shopping. In the **Cathedral**, you can pause for a while, before you enjoy dinner in the quaint **Old Grammar School** *(19 St Mary's Street | tel. 01872 27 85 59 | www.theoldgrammarschool.com | Moderate).*

Leave Truro **on the A39 heading south to ⑪ Falmouth → p. 33** where you can listen to old mariners' tales at the **National Maritime Museum**. Around midday you should continue **via Trescobeas Road and Hillhead Road to the ⑫ Lizard Peninsula → p. 37**. Start at the **Lizard Lighthouse** on a **short hike heading west on the South West Coast Path.** After a while you can see **Lizard Point**, England's southernmost point. Stop for lunch here at **Polpeor Café**. Carry on along the coastal path as far as **Kynance Cove**, a romantic bay. Take off your shoes and go paddling in the water! You can also go for a swim here. Then, head for the **Mullion Cove Hotel** with its stunning sea views.

You leave Lizard **along the coast heading west (A8083, A394). At Marazion** you will notice ⑬ **St Michael's Mount → p. 41** in the water. At low tide, you can walk across and enjoy the island setting. At high tide, boats will ferry you back. Then, for two nights **head to nearby ⑭ Penzance → p. 40**. The harbour city offers the attractive **Jubilee Pool** where you can swim in the Art Deco outdoor pool with a view across the bay.

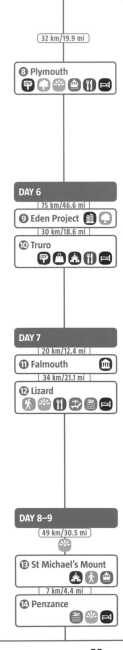

32 km/19.9 mi

⑧ Plymouth

**DAY 6**

75 km/46.6 mi

⑨ Eden Project

30 km/18.6 mi

⑩ Truro

**DAY 7**

20 km/12.4 mi

⑪ Falmouth

34 km/21.1 mi

⑫ Lizard

**DAY 8–9**

49 km/30.5 mi

⑬ St Michael's Mount

7 km/4.4 mi

⑭ Penzance

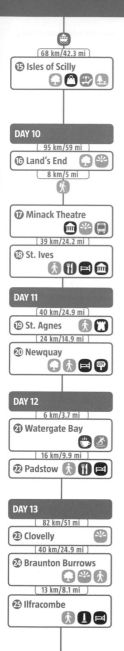

68 km/42.3 mi

**⑮ Isles of Scilly**

---

**DAY 10**

95 km/59 mi

**⑯ Land's End**

8 km/5 mi

**⑰ Minack Theatre**

39 km/24.2 mi

**⑱ St. Ives**

---

**DAY 11**

40 km/24.9 mi

**⑲ St. Agnes**

24 km/14.9 mi

**⑳ Newquay**

---

**DAY 12**

6 km/3.7 mi

**㉑ Watergate Bay**

16 km/9.9 mi

**㉒ Padstow**

---

**DAY 13**

82 km/51 mi

**㉓ Clovelly**

40 km/24.9 mi

**㉔ Braunton Burrows**

13 km/8.1 mi

**㉕ Ilfracombe**

---

At 9.15am the *Scillonian III* docks in the harbour to take you on a **day trip to the ⑮ Isles of Scilly → p. 35.** There is only enough time to visit **St Mary's**, but it is well worth exploring with its small capital **Hugh Town**. How about some fresh fruit from the **Farm Deli Store** (*Hugh Street*) for a picnic on the beach? At 4.30pm the boat departs for Penzance.

England's westernmost point **⑯ Land's End → p. 42 (accessible from the A30)** is on today's schedule. Leave the tourist crowds behind and head off on a **hike (7 km/4.4 mi) along the coast to ⑰ Minack Theatre → p. 43,** Cornwall's amazing open-air theatre with breathtaking sea views. **From the car park at Porthcurno, take the bus service 1A back to Land's End** and your car. **Carry on via the A30 and B3306 to ⑱ St Ives → p. 45,** Cornwall's artists' haven where you can enjoy a stroll by the quayside, dinner and stopover.

In the morning visit the **Tate Gallery**, a branch of London's famous museum, before you **carry on via the A30 to ⑲ St Agnes**, once the centre of tin mining: take a stroll and by the coast you will notice **Wheal Coates → p. 43**, the ruin of a pump house. In early afternoon, you should **continue the A307 to ⑳ Newquay → p. 39**, where you can take a short walk along the beach before a good night's sleep.

After breakfast, explore Newquay. **Drive along the B3276 and stop at ㉑ Watergate Bay** where you can stop for a coffee, or have a go on a surf board at the **Extreme Academy. You can enjoy the food in ㉒ Padstow → p. 56:** TV chef Rick Stein serves fresh fish here. After you have explored the romantic harbour town, this is a great way to finish the day.

In the morning, you head **onto the A389 and A39 to ㉓ Clovelly → p. 83**, a picture postcard fishing village in Devon with sea views. At **Clovelly Pottery** (*summer daily 11am–5pm | Lower Yard | tel. 01237 43 10 05 | short.travel/cod6*) you can make your own vase! **Past the sand dunes at ㉔ Braunton Burrows**, where you can get out and breathe in the fresh air, **you carry on to your overnight accommodation in ㉕ Ilfracombe → p. 83.** Another harbour town with a unique attraction: the artist, Damien Hirst, created the controversial, 20 m/65.6 ft high bronze statue called **Verity**.

Via the A361 and A3123 you head back on the A39 as far as Exmoor. The beautiful and rugged countryside is eye catching thanks to its coastline. First, explore ㉖ Lynton/Lynmouth → p. 79, the twin town with the old water-powered **Cliff Railway**. Then, **continue driving to ㉗ Porlock** → p. 80. Here you should visit the coffee roastery **DJ Miles** which also sells delicious tea varieties as well as fabulous coffee. **Via Tiverton you head back on the A396 for the return trip to ❶ Exeter.**

**DAY 14**

29 km/18 mi

㉖ Lynton/Lynmouth

20 km/12.4 mi

㉗ Porlock

85 km/52.8 mi

❶ Exeter

---

## ② ON THE TRAIL OF AGATHA CHRISTIE

| START: ❶ Torquay Museum, Torquay <br> END: ⑫ Grand Hotel, Torquay | 1 day <br> Walking time <br> (without stops) <br> approx. 1 ½ hours |
|---|---|
| Distance: <br> ➔ 5.5 km/3.4 mi plus journey to Greenway | |

**COSTS:** £60/person for food, admissions, train rides
**WHAT TO PACK:** comfortable shoes, rain gear, sun protection in summer, warm clothes (even in summer)

**IMPORTANT TIPS:** Dartmouth Steam Railway *(www.dartmouthrail river.co.uk)* from Paignton to ⑪ Greenway: check the timetable! You must also tell the conductor that you want to alight at Greenway.

---

On this tour, you learn about the different episodes in the life of Agatha Christie. England's most famous writer of crime thrillers was born in 1890 in Torquay.

The doyenne of English crime novels, Agatha Christie

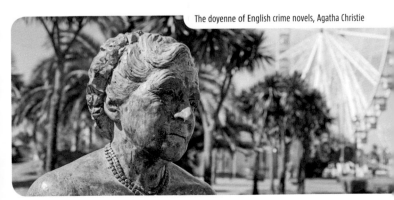

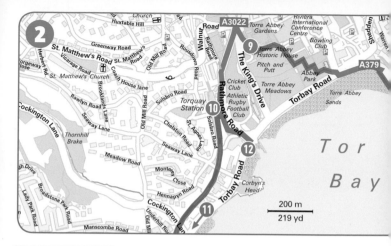

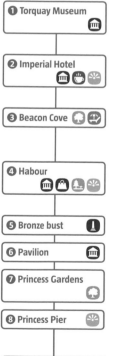

**1 Torquay Museum** 🏛️

**2 Imperial Hotel** 🏛️☕🌸

**3 Beacon Cove** 🎧🔀

**4 Habour** 🏛️🛍️🛥️🌸

**5 Bronze bust** ❶

**6 Pavilion** 🏛️

**7 Princess Gardens** 🌳

**8 Princess Pier** 🌸

**9 Torre Abbey** 🏰🎧

**10:00am** Start at the **1 Torquay Museum** *(summer daily, otherwise Mon–Sat 10am–4pm | 529 Babbacombe Road | www.torquaymuseum.org)* which has a small section dedicated to Agatha Christie. **Via Parkhill Road** you arrive at the **2 Imperial Hotel → p. 75** where Christie supposedly enjoyed afternoon tea. The hotel is featured in several of her novels. During tea in the **restaurant** you can enjoy the view over Torquay. **On the way to the harbour** you will pass **3 Beacon Cove** where, INSIDER TIP like Agatha Christie, you can paddle in the water.

Stroll onwards to the **4 harbour**, where many buildings still date to the writer's era. Order a coffee and sandwich in one of the cafés. Relax and enjoy the views of the boats! **Behind the Tourist Information office at Cary Parade** is a **5 bronze bust** of Agatha Christie. In the **6 Pavilion**, Agatha and Archie Christie once listened to a Wagner concert – the date culminated in a marriage proposal. **Now, walk to the 7 Princess Gardens** – they feature in the novel "The A.B.C. Murders" – the detour is worth it to see the exotic plants. **Immediately opposite, at 8 Princess Pier**, Christie used to go roller skating. Enjoy a stroll to the end of the pier.

Murder can be so easy: many of the victims in Christie's books were killed by poisons from exotic plants. In the garden of **9 Torre Abbey → p. 74** there is a special

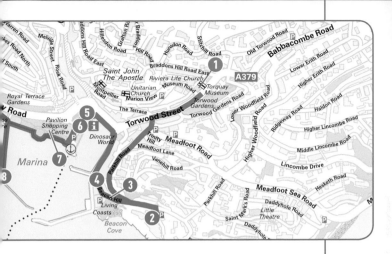

area dedicated to poisonous plants. **From the nearby ⑩ train station at Torquay, now continue to the neighbouring town of Paignton → p. 75.**

`02:00pm` Take the Dartmouth Steam Railway and travel just like in Miss Marple's day **from Paignton to ⑪ Greenway → p. 64. A bus takes you from the train stop to the country estate.** Welcome to the home of Agatha Christie: Greenway was for many years the writer's summer residence. You can not only admire the house with many of her personal items – the view from the gardens across the River Dart is fantastic. Before you leave, you should enjoy a cider or cream tea at the small **Barn Café**. At 4pm you then head to **Dartmouth by boat → p. 63**. Here, you must **cross to the other side at Kingswear → p. 65** to catch the last **train back to Paignton** at 5pm. From here, you can take the **train back to Torquay**.

`06:00pm` **Immediately opposite the station** you will see the ⑫ **Grand Hotel** *(Torbay Road | tel. 01803 29 66 77 | www.grandtorquay.co.uk | Expensive)*. During dinner, you can enjoy the view of the bay of Torbay and imagine how it must have been to be Agatha Christie: the doyenne of crime spent one night in this hotel on her honeymoon in 1914.

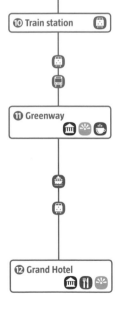

⑩ Train station

⑪ Greenway

⑫ Grand Hotel

# HIKING ON THE SOUTH WEST COAST PATH

| | |
|---|---|
| **START:** ❶ Newquay bus station<br>**END:** ❼ Great Western Hotel, Newquay | **1 day**<br>Walking time<br>(without stops)<br>approx. 4 ½ hours |
| **Distance:**<br>➡ 16 km/9.9 mi plus bus ride from Newquay | |

**COSTS:** £45/person for food and bus tickets
**WHAT TO PACK:** hiking gear, rain gear, hat, sun protection

**IMPORTANT TIPS:** Bus A5 from ❶ Bus station, Newquay: please check the timetable *(www.firstgroup.com/cornwall)*, buses are not frequent on this route.
❸ Bedruthan Steps: please be aware of the heavy surf here, the bay is only accessible at low tide. The steps are closed in winter. The restaurant Fifteen in ❻ Watergate Bay is only open until 2.30pm. The symbol for the coastal path is a white acorn on a brown background.

Cornwall's coastline is impressive! The South West Coast Path is a circular coastal route. On this section, you can explore the amazing Bedruthan Steps.

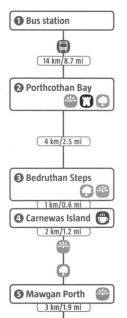

❶ Bus station

14 km/8.7 mi

❷ Porthcothan Bay

4 km/2.5 mi

❸ Bedruthan Steps

1 km/0.6 mi

❹ Carnewas Island

2 km/1.2 mi

❺ Mawgan Porth

3 km/1.9 mi

**08:45am** From the ❶ **bus station** in **Newquay** → p. 39 hop on the **A5 bus to start the hiking tour. Get off at Porthcothan Bay. At the red telephone box carry on along the path in the direction of** *Stores*. Now you are already on the South West Coast Path. **Carry on towards the coast:** the romantic rugged coastline at ❷ **Porthcothan Bay** is your first photo stop. **Now carry on heading south-west**, keeping the sea on your right-hand side. Close to the path you will notice six burial barrows which date to the Bronze Age. You can also discover exotic plants: Cornish mallow with pink flowers, yellow flowering golden samphire and pink beach lilac. **Carry on always following the coastline. Before the bay at Park Head you are already getting closer to the** ❸ **Bedruthan Steps** → p. 40: the free-standing rocks seem to emerge from the rugged coastline. In summer, a narrow path leads down to the beach. **At the National Trust car park** ❹ **Carnewas Island** there is time to stop at the **café** *(March–Oct daily)*. Enjoy a nice cup of tea! **You head back along the coast path continuing in a south-westerly direction**. You will enjoy the view between the rocky coastline and green countryside inland. At ❺ **Mawgan Porth** you will notice the first surfer crowds.

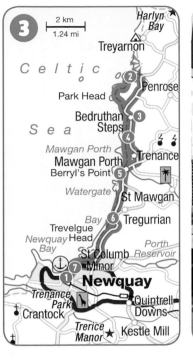

Jamie Oliver's exclusive restaurant
*Fifteen* at Watergate Bay near Newquay

**01:00pm** It's time for lunch. In ⑥ **Watergate Bay** you can stop at Jamie Oliver's restaurant **Fifteen → p. 40** with a romantic view across the bay. Afterwards, you can enjoy a dip in the sea. **Carry on and continue on the South West Coast Path**. The area is starting to get busier. In the distance, you can already see the first buildings in Newquay. Don't miss the opportunity for a last glance at the natural rocky coastline – in Newquay the views are obscured by buildings.

**03:00pm** At Porth Beach in Newquay the coast path joins normal roads along some sections. **Continue towards the station. Shortly beforehand, turn left where Narrowcliff turns into Cliff Road you will see the** ⑦ **Great Western Hotel** *(Cliff Road | www.greatwesternnewquay.co.uk)*. The hotel has a INSIDER TIP terrace with a fabulous view over Great Western Beach – the perfect spot to relax with a Pimms and lemonade!

⑥ **Watergate Bay**

5 km/3.1 mi

⑦ **Great Western Hotel**

# CASTLES & GARDENS

**START:** ❶ Lost Gardens of Heligan
**END:** ❼ Bovey Castle

**Distance:**
🚗 225 km/140 mi

2 days
Driving time
(without stops)
3 ½ hours

**COSTS:** £250–450/person for overnight stay in a double room, admissions, food, petrol
**WHAT TO PACK:** hiking shoes, rain gear, sun protection

**IMPORTANT TIPS:** : In winter, some palaces and gardens are closed. Several houses and gardens are owned by the National Trust, and you can save the admission fee with a 7 day pass *(www.visitbritain shop.com)*.

Magnificent country houses, old palaces and vast gardens – some of England's most spectacular sights are to be found in Devon and Cornwall. This car tour includes them.

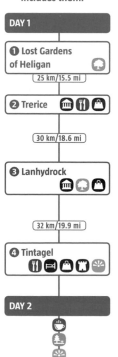

**DAY 1**

❶ Lost Gardens
of Heligan

25 km/15.5 mi

❷ Trerice

30 km/18.6 mi

❸ Lanhydrock

32 km/19.9 mi

❹ Tintagel

**DAY 2**

Start in the ❶ **Lost Gardens of Heligan →** p. 44, a magnificent garden dating back to the 18th century. Explore the glasshouses and the jungle with its numerous subtropical plants! Carry on **via the B3287 and A390 to ❷ Trerice →** p. 40, a typical Elizabethan manor house. The Dutch gable facade is unique. After a tour of the building you can enjoy lunch in the **Barn Restaurant**. Browse in the **shop** where you can also buy garden plants to take home.

**Head onto the A3058 to drive to the A30 to travel east.**
❸ **Lanhydrock →** p. 51 is also a country house that was originally a monastery. It is surrounded by a magnificent garden and large park. A tour of the house explains how the staff and owners lived in the past. In the **shop**, you can buy delicious shortbread from Cornwall to enjoy on the road! **Via the A39 continue to ❹ Tintagel →** p. 57 which is famous for its supposed connection to King Arthur. In the **Camelot Castle Hotel**, you can stopover by the coast. Relax and feel like a lord over dinner.

Early next morning set off in the car to **the ruins of Tintagel Castle**. On the way, you can stop and stock up with fresh Caffè latte and Danish pastries at the **Cornish Bakery** – perfect for a picnic at the castle with

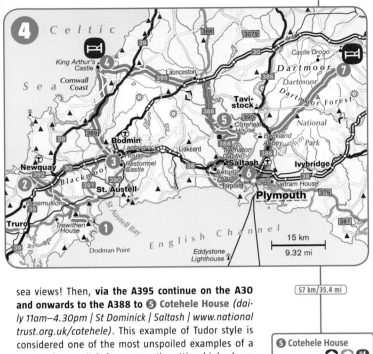

sea views! Then, **via the A395 continue on the A30 and onwards to the A388 to ⑤ Cotehele House** (*daily 11am–4.30pm | St Dominick | Saltash | www.national trust.org.uk/cotehele*). This example of Tudor style is considered one of the most unspoiled examples of a country house. It is in a romantic setting high above the Tamar River and the garden is a show of colourful flowers depending on the season. Enjoy lunch at **Edgcumbe Tea Room** by the river. **On the A388 and A38 it is not far to ⑥ Antony** (*May–Aug Tue–Thu, Sat/Sun 12.30pm–4.30pm | Torpoint | www.national trust.org.uk/antony*). The country house is famous for its portrait collection and the modern sculpture garden. After a tour, you can relax and enjoy a cream tea in the **café**.

Now it's time to set off for your overnight accommodation: carry on **along the A386 and B3212 across Dartmoor**. Enjoy the scenic countryside on both sides of the route until you arrive in the north-west at ⑦ **Bovey Castle → p. 62**, an exclusive golf hotel in a former country house. Here, you can relax from your sightseeing tour in the swimming pool and enjoy some pampering in the spa.

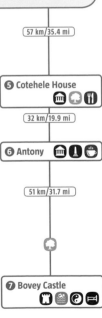

57 km/35.4 mi

⑤ Cotehele House

32 km/19.9 mi

⑥ Antony

51 km/31.7 mi

⑦ Bovey Castle

# SPORTS & ACTIVITIES

In Devon and Cornwall, sports are incredibly popular: especially rugby, football, cricket and of course – water sports. People are very active here.

The craze for jogging and fitness has long since reached the south-west of the country – fitness studios have sprung up everywhere and every morning you will notice cheerful people out for a run.

In Devon and Cornwall, surfing is a traditional sport and swimming in the sea is so convenient that many people have already taken up this activity. Tennis and golf are national sports – expensive club memberships are no longer required to enjoy these activities.

## COASTEERING

This adventure sport basically involves exploring rocky cliffs that are otherwise difficult to access. In a wetsuit and helmet, you climb the rocks, jump into the sea, swim into small caves and make the ascent again. This amazing sport should only be tried in groups (£35 to £50 per person) – it is too dangerous for novices to try. You can have a go at this sport in plenty of coastal resorts, including Land's End, Salcombe and on the Isles of Scilly. *Information: www.coasteering.org*

## CYCLING

The cycle network covers 23,700 km/ 14,726 mi and most of the routes are in

## Surfing, hiking and cycling: adventure sports in Devon and Cornwall offer fantastic experiences

Devon and Cornwall. They often head through amazing countryside such as the *Camel Trail* near Padstow and *Granite Way* near Lydford. There is a cycle hire shop in most tourist resorts (approx. £20 per day). *Information: www.sustrans.org.uk*

### DIVING

The coastline is dotted with thousands of shipwrecks. There are about 3,500 shipwrecks off the Cornish coast alone.

The bad weather, conflicts and reefs have made their mark over the centuries. While this is bad news for shipping, it offers plenty of adventures for divers. Despite the often cold water, diving remains a popular sport here. The Isles of Scilly are popular diving areas – about 1,000 shipwrecks are located here and between Bude and Hartland there is a similar number. *Information about the best diving locations: www.ukdiving.co.uk*

## FISHING

You can also go fishing wherever fish is served: the rivers and lakes are full of trout and sometimes even salmon. To cast a line here you need a *rod license* that angling clubs, the authorities and post offices can issue (depending on the type of fish from £5 per day).
The South West Lakes Trust *(www.sw lakesfishing.co.uk)* maintains a number of lakes and issues licences for them. No license is required for sea fishing. In many ports, special half-day and day tours are available for keen anglers. *Information: www.anglingtrust.net*

## HIKING

The south west is a paradise for hikers. In addition to the *South West Coast Path (www.southwestcoastpath.org.uk)*, a circular coast path between Devon and Cornwall, there are numerous smaller signposted routes in the counties, particularly on Exmoor and Dartmoor. During the winter you should pack sufficient supplies, as the coastal cafés and kiosks are generally closed in this season. You can join organised hiking tours almost everywhere, contact the local tourist information offices for more details. You are unlikely to encounter any danger – except (very rare) adders and (more often) cows that you should make a wide detour around.

## RIDING

On Exmoor and Dartmoor horses are part of the scenery. Several hotels and B&Bs offer riding holidays, and you can also join in short riding tours here. *(www.bhsaccess.org.uk/ridemaps)*. *Information: www.bhs.org.uk | www.visit-exmoor.co.uk/horse-riding*

## SAILING

Most traditional sailing venues are along the south coast, generally towards Hampshire and Sussex. South Devon and Cornwall are also popular with many sailors. Fowey and Dartmouth are classic sailing centres as well as the Isles of Scilly. The main regattas are the *Torbay Royal Regatta, Falmouth Week Regatta* as well as the *Port of Dartmouth Royal Regatta* (all during August). *Information: www.rya.org.uk*

## STAND-UP PADDLING

Surfing has long been part of Cornish identity. However, recently some people also like to take their paddle boards with them. For *Stand up Paddle Boarding* you do not need a sail, instead you paddle along – and sooner or later you will fall into the water. You can now learn *Stand up Paddle Boarding* in almost all major surfing centres in south-west England. You can also hire wetsuits and equipment. For more information visit the British Stand Up Paddling Association's website. *(www.bsupa.org.uk)*.

## SURFING

Newquay is one of the top surfing centres in Europe thanks to its long beaches and fabulous surf conditions. Sennen Cove in Cornwall and Bigbury in Devon are also popular with surfers. Almost all major beaches offer surf boards and wetsuits for hire (about £10) as well as courses for all abilities (from £30). *Information: www.surfingengland.org | www.surfing-cornwall.com*

## TENNIS

Tennis has always been in fashion but

since Andy Murray's success, many people are glued to the TV watching even more tennis tournaments. And who doesn't like to play? Many larger hotels joy a spot of pampering. More and more hotels are opening spa centres that are generally also open to non-residents for a fee. There are head and neck massages

Simply glorious: hiking along the Cornish coast and on the South West Coast Path

have tennis courts. The campaign ● **INSIDER TIP** *Tennis for Free (www.tennisforfree.com)* aims to provide as many tennis courts and courses as possible free of charge.

There are two courses so far in Devon – once a week in Exeter and Plymouth. *Information: www.tennishub.co.uk*

## SPA TREATMENTS

In Devon and Cornwall, you can easily en-

as well as an increasing number of various Asian massage offers. Larger hotels often offer a sauna and steam bath, as well as a pool, which is an essential part of a spa package and offers more than just warm water. After a swim you can enjoy the pampering – and you should take your time. Several websites give details of reasonably priced spa packages, although these are often only available on fixed dates *(www.spafinder.co.uk | www.spabreaks.com)*.

# TRAVEL WITH KIDS

In Devon and Cornwall children are most welcome and with the many fun activities on offer it's easy to keep them entertained.

Many hotels, restaurants and museums cater for younger visitors and have special offers for them – including special menus, drawing equipment and toys. Many popular attractions offer tailormade packages for families with children. Near beaches, you can almost always find a surfing hire centre which offers courses for kids.

The prices for family tickets at the following attractions are generally for two adults and two children when you buy the tickets on site. You can save money at almost all tourist venues if you book tickets online in advance from the relevant websites.

WEST CORNWALL

### FLAMBARDS EXPERIENCE
(127 D5) (*ⓜ D11*)

Fun and entertainment anytime: the small theme park near Helston not only offers carousels, go-karts and the Skyraker ride but also parts of the *Concorde* prototype including the cockpit. *April–Oct daily 10am–5pm, Nov–March (only indoors) Tue–Thu 10am–4pm | family admission from £75, indoor attractions from £37 | Clodgey Lane | Helston | www.flambards.co.uk*

### LAPPA VALLEY STEAM RAILWAY
(122 A5) (*ⓜ E9*)

This 3 km/1.9 mi steam railway near Newquay originally serviced a local mine. Now, it is a leisure park with steam

**Fun and entertainment galore: water slides, steam train rides and a rope park. Even dinosaurs join in**

engines. You can also go canoeing on the lake and much more. *April–Oct daily 9.30am–5.10pm, Nov and Feb/March Sat/Sun 11.10am–3.50 pm | Family ticket £40 | Benny Halt | St Newlyn East near Newquay | www.lappavalley.co.uk*

**NEWQUAY ZOO** (122 A4) *(∅ E8)*
With numerous awards for sustainable tourism, Newquay Zoo is home to many rare animals. Over 130 species are found here including lions, monkeys and penguins. *April–Oct daily 10am–5pm, Nov–March 10am–4pm | family admission from £45.50 | Trenance Gardens | www.newquayzoo.org.uk*

**WATERWORLD** ● (122 A4) *(∅ E8)*
On rainy days, and if it's too cold in the sea – at this leisure pool in Newquay the kids can swim, slide and splash about in the fountains in warm water heated to about 30° C/86° F. There is also a 25 m/82 ft slide for adults.
*Mon–Fri 7am–9pm, Sat/Sun 8am–5.30pm | family admission from £25 |*

*Trenance Leisure Park | Newquay | www.
tempusleisure.org.uk*

## EAST CORNWALL

**ADRENALIN QUARRY** (123 E4) (*∭ J8*)
Jump from a 50 m/164 ft clifftop and
travel at 60 km/h/37 mph on a zip line
over a 500 m/1,640 ft high ravine – this
park is perfect for all adrenalin junkies! If
you weigh between 25 kg/55 lbs and 115
kg/254 lbs you can join in – there are no
age restrictions. You need plenty of cou-
rage but you also wear a safety harness.
*April–Sept daily 10am–6pm, Oct–March
Sat/Sun 10am–5pm | Lower Clicker Road |
Menheniot near Liskeard | family admissi-
on from £50 | www.adrenalinquarry.co.uk*

### HIDDEN VALLEY DISCOVERY PARK
(123 E2) (*∭ J6*)
It may not be an exceptional park, but it
offers great entertainment. Children can
solve puzzles here on the trail of Sherlock
Holmes, or cross a maze and discover se-
cret doors as well as enjoying a ride on
a miniature steam train. *April–Sept daily
10am–5pm | family admission from £38 |
Tredidon | St. Thomas | Launceston | www.
hiddenvalleydiscoverypark.co.uk*

### POLPERRO MODEL VILLAGE
(123 D5) (*∭ H9*)
Polperro in miniature: this traditional
miniature wonderland recreates the real
village on a smaller scale. Children can
wander among the houses and enjoy
the attractions to learn about local his-
tory. *April–Oct daily 10am–6pm | family
admission £10 | The Old Forge | Mill Hill |
Polperro | www.polperromodelvillage.com*

### TRETHORNE LEISURE PARK
(123 E2) (*∭ J6*)
You can hold a lamb in your arms, or ride
on the dodgems – children can run wild,

play and get closer to all kinds of animals
at this small leisure park. Enjoy a game
of miniature *crazy golf*, or at the *climb-
ing frame* children can climb up a small
wall, obviously wearing a safety harness.
*April–Oct daily, Nov–March Sat/Sun 10am–
6pm | family admission from £44 | Ken-
nards House | Launceston | www.trethorne
leisure.com*

## SOUTH DEVON

**DEVON RAILWAY CENTRE**
(120 B3–4) (*∭ O4*)
A whole park dedicated to railways!
Children can ride on a miniature train
and play the signal man as well as stamp
tickets. A miniature park and railway ex-
hibition offer indoor adventure. *April–
Sept daily 10.30am–5pm | family ad-
mission £27.90 | A396, Bickleigh | www.
devonrailwaycentre.co.uk*

### GO APE! (120 B6) (*∭ O6*)
Hangout like a monkey: at this park
near Exeter, you can go zip trekking
and hangout until you're breathless.
The only condition: visitors must be
at least ten years old and at 1.40 m/
4.6 ft tall. *April–Oct daily 9am–5pm,
Feb/March and Nov Sat/Sun 9am–4pm
(in good weather – it is recommended to
check the website beforehand!) | admis-
sion for adults from £33, children £25 |
Haldon Forest Park | Bullers Hill | Kenn-
ford | www.goape.co.uk*

### SPLASHDOWN QUAYWEST ☀
(125 E4) (*∭ O8*)
The biggest outdoor waterpark in Britain offers plenty of attractions with
eight waterslides and spectacular
views. *May–Sept daily 9am–5pm | ad-
mission £15 per person | Tanners Road |
Goodrington Sands | Paignton | www.
splashdownwaterparks.co.uk/quaywest*

A dinosaur in Devon? At Woodlands leisure park, of course!

### WOODLANDS (125 D5) (*N9*)

Devon's largest theme park is ideal for families with giant swingboats and slides. The park has special zones for animals and dinosaur trails. *April–Oct daily, Nov–March Sat/Sun 9.30am–5pm | prices vary throughout the season – check website for details | Woodlands Leisure Park | Blackawton | Totnes | www.woodlandspark.com*

## NORTH DEVON

### THE BIG SHEEP (118 C3) (*K3*)

Once this was an ordinary farm and now it is a large family theme park. The sheep are still the stars but the attractions also feature other animals, such as swan pedalos, piggy pull along and much more. There are also live animals! *April–Oct daily, Nov–March Sat/Sun 10am–5pm | admission per person £13.95 | Abbotsham near Bideford | www.thebigsheep.co.uk*

### THE CRAFT HUT (118 C1–2) (*K1*)

The kids can get creative here: you can paint your own pottery such as small animals, mugs and dinosaurs. When the pottery is fired, you collect the items to take home with you. *Feb–Oct daily 10am–5pm | Sandy Lane | Woolacombe*

### THE MILKY WAY ADVENTURE PARK (118 B4) (*J3*)

This is not about chocolate bars, but about the galaxy. There are several rides, a miniature train and plenty of sci-fi exhibitions to offer guaranteed entertainment. *April–Oct daily, Nov–March Sat/Sun 10am–5pm | family admission £57.80 | Downland Farm | Higher Clovelly | Clovelly | www.themilkyway.co.uk*

# FESTIVALS & EVENTS

The weather in Devon and Cornwall is often mild, so people like to celebrate outdoors. There is always something happening from regattas to food festivals. Even in winter: there are Christmas markets in almost all larger towns. German markets are now popular with *mulled wine and Bratwurst sausage*. One of the best is the INSIDER TIP Christmas Market near Exeter Cathedral.

## FESTIVALS

### JANUARY

*Science Weekends at Eden:* For three weekends in January, the *Eden Project* offers special science weekends. *www.edenproject.com*

### FEBRUARY

*St Ives Feast:* Once a year, St Ives revives the old tradition of *Hurling the Silver Ball*, an early version of rugby.

### MARCH

*St Piran's Day:* On or near 5 March everyone in Cornwall remembers St Piran, the patron saint of the county. For example, there are parades in Falmouth, Bodmin and Redruth.

### APRIL

*Porthleven Food and Music Festival:* A long weekend at the end of April with plenty of specialities and music from Gospel to Electro. *www.porthlevenfoodfestival.com* It's all about local produce at the ◉ *Exeter Festival of Southwest food and drink*. *www.exeterfoodanddrinkfestival.co.uk*

### MAY

The *Fowey Festival of Arts and Literature* is inspired by the writer Daphne du Maurier. *www.foweyfestival.com*

### JUNE

*Brixham Trawler Race:* Fishing trawlers line up to race in Brixham harbour.
*Lemonfest:* Rock festival in Newton Abbot. *www.lemonfest.co.uk*

### JULY

*Rock Oyster Festival:* In the village of Rock, in early July, everything revolves around oysters. *www.rockoysterfestival.co.uk*
*Looe Carnival:* Looe celebrates carnival for an entire week.

### AUGUST

*Regattas:* The major sailing competitions are all held in August, including in Fowey, Torbay, Dartmouth and Salcombe.

**Shaldon Water Carnival:** A carnival on boats in Shaldon. *www.shaldonwater carnival.co.uk*

### SEPTEMBER

**St Ives September Festival:** September in St Ives is a celebration of music and art. *www.stivesseptemberfestival.co.uk*

**Fish Stock Brixham:** A festival all about fish dishes in Brixham. *www.fishstock brixham.co.uk*

**Agatha Christie Festival:** Torquay commemorates the famous crime thriller writer with an annual literature festival. *www.agathachristiefestival.com*

### OCTOBER

**Two Moors Festival:** One of the major festivals for classical music in England – the venues are Exmoor and Dartmoor. *www.thetwomoorsfestival.co.uk*

### NOVEMBER

**Tar Barrels:** On 5 November in Ottery St Mary burning barrels are carried through the streets. *www.tarbarrels. co.uk*

**Ilfracombe rocks:** Music festival in Ilfracombe with many independent bands. *www.ilfracomberocksfestivals.co.uk*

### DECEMBER

**Padstow Christmas Festival:** At the Christmas festival in the gourmet fishing port of Padstow you obviously have a wide choice of food. *www.padstow christmasfestival.co.uk*

**INSIDER TIP** *Mousehole Christmas Lights:* From mid-December, the lights are switched on and illuminate the harbour with a festive glow. *www.mouseholelights.org.uk*

## PUBLIC HOLIDAYS

| | |
|---|---|
| 1 January | New Year's Day |
| 30 March 2018, 19 April 2019, 10 April 2020 | Good Friday |
| 2 April 2018, 22 April 2019, 13 April 2020 | Easter Monday |
| 23 April | St George's Day |
| First Monday in May | May Day Holiday |
| Last Monday in May | Spring Bank Holiday |
| Last Monday in August | Summer Bank Holiday |
| 25 December | Christmas Day |
| 26 December | Boxing Day |

# LINKS, BLOGS, APPS & MORE

LINKS & BLOGS

agathachristie.wikia.com A small Wiki about Agatha Christie and her fictional characters with background information, pictures and much more.

www.thegoodpubguide.co.uk The reference guide for pub lovers: the "Good Pub Guide" lists the country's best pubs – many of them are also in Devon and Cornwall.

www.nomadicmatt.com/travel-blogs/cornwall The motto of best-selling author Nomadic Matt is: travel better, cheaper, longer. He has also visited Cornwall and shares his impressions of this trip – and many others – in his blog.

www.bbc.com/news/england/cornwall BBC Cornwall local news and traffic service.

www.foodfromcornwall.co.uk A site about food from Cornwall with numerous recipes for local specialities.

www.firstgroup.com/cornwall A site run by the national bus company that also operates the local transport service in many towns in Cornwall. You can research the online timetables and routes.

short.travel/cod1 A site with essential information for a holiday on Dartmoor: the British Army uses parts of the national park for exercises and manoeuvres. This website provides details about firing schedules when you must avoid the area.

Regardless of whether you are still researching your trip or already in Devon and Cornwall: these addresses will provide you with more information, videos and networks to make your holiday even more enjoyable.

VIDEOS & MUSIC

vimeo.com/tag:rick+stein A site that features videos with Cornwall's famous chef Rick Stein.

www.visitcornwall.tv A site with a collection of videos about Cornwall, cycle routes, locations, festivals and coastal areas.

www.bbc.co.uk/radiocornwall Listen live to the local BBC radio station for Cornwall online. *www.bbc.co.uk/radiodevon*

short.travel/cod2 The official video channel for Visit Cornwall on YouTube.

www.youtube.com/user/DartmoorNPA A site featuring films from and about Dartmoor.

short.travel/cod3 A video with numerous surf shots from Newquay.

short.travel/cod4 The YouTube channel for Jamie Oliver's restaurant Fifteen with videos starring some trainee chefs as well as recipes.

APPS

English Heritage Days Out You can search for and locate the attractions and castles owned by English Heritage (Android, Amazon, iOS).

Met Office The free app from the official weather station, the Met Office, is indispensable for planning your day – especially for excursions in the countryside (Android and iOS).

National Trust The National Trust has a user-friendly app that enables you to search for local attractions and nationwide (Android, iOS, Windows).

Sky WiFi Finder This app enables you to find free WiFi zones and The Cloud near you (Android, iOS).

Trainline The perfect app for train travel – not only searches timetables, but helps you to buy the cheapest ticket online (Android, Amazon, iOS).

UK Tides An app that allows you to search for tide times in locations in Britain (Android). Similar apps are also available for iOS (e.g. "AnyTide UK") and Windows ("Tide").

# TRAVEL TIPS

## ACCOMMODATION

### BED & BREAKFAST (B&B)

Small guesthouses or private house-holders who rent a room in their home have recognised for a long while how much to charge for an overnight stay. Generally, you can expect to pay from £40 per person. B&B means literally a bed and breakfast – you usually avoid staying in the room during the daytime and allow your hosts some privacy.

### CAMPING

Camping anywhere in the countryside is not allowed in England, although it is often tolerated, if you clear every-thing away. There are official camp sites everywhere, some have pubs and high quality washrooms. Tourist Information offices offer plenty of advice as well as the *Camping & Caravanning Club (www. campingandcaravanningclub.co.uk).*

## RESPONSIBLE TRAVEL

It doesn't take a lot to be environ-mentally friendly whilst travelling. Don't just think about your carbon footprint whilst flying to and from your holiday destination but also about how you can protect nature and culture abroad. As a tourist, it is especially important to respect nature, look out for local products, cycle instead of driving, save water and much more. If you would like to find out more about eco-tourism please visit: *www.ecotourism.org*

### HOLIDAY APARTMENTS

The growing popularity of holiday home accommodation means that the previous expensive prices and relative lack of choice has been transformed with entire holiday apartment com-plexes offering more and more luxu-rious accommodation, which is also available for daily or weekly rates. The major providers are *Holiday Lettings (www.holidaylettings.co.uk)*, *Hoseasons (www.hoseasons.co.uk)* and *Airbnb (*www.airbnb.com).

A pleasant alternative is the National Trust *(tel. 0344 8 00 20 70 (*) | www. nationaltrustholidays.org.uk)* which also rents out rooms and holiday apartments or even entire cottages on its country estates. The same applies for the Land-mark Trust *(tel. 01628 82 59 25 | www. landmarktrust.org.uk)* which specialises in the rental of listed monuments, in-cluding lighthouses and cottages.

### HOTELS

Hotels are available for all types of budget and taste. From small, family run hotels to international chains – there is something for everyone. Some of the older grand hotels have now been converted into chic boutique hotels and more and more budget hotels are opening.

### YOUTH HOSTELS

Youth hostels have overcome their poor reputation and now also offer double rooms. The official body is the *Youth Hos-tel Association (YHA | Trevelyan House | Dimple Road | Matlock | tel. 01629 59 27 00 | www.yha.org.uk).* In holiday locations, there are now also private hostels for young people.

# From arrival to weather

Your holiday from start to finish: the most important addresses and information for your trip to Devon and Cornwall

## ARRIVAL

🚗 If you are coming from abroad, the Eurotunnel is the quickest way to cross the English Channel, although it is usually the most expensive. The car train departs every 20 to 40 minutes depending on the time of day from Calais in France to Folkestone in England. The crossing lasts about 25 minutes. Per vehicle and trip from £79. *www.euro tunnel.com*

🚆 The Eurostar fast train service also travels through the Eurotunnel and connects Paris and Brussels with London St Pancras (journey time approx. 2 hours). There are connections from Germany via Frankfurt. From London, the journey times are 2 hours to Exeter and 5 hours to Penzance. Please note: the trains to Devon and Cornwall depart from a different station than the Eurostar, i.e. Paddington Station. The Night Riviera Sleeper is a popular service *(from £100 per person in a double berth | www.gwr.com)*, a night train to Penzance.

⛴ The quickest route from mainland Europe by ferry is from Calais (1.5 hours) or Dunkirk (2 hours) to Dover with DFDS *(www.dfdsseaways.com)* and P&O *(www.poferries.com)*, from about £35 per crossing.
Other ferry crossings: Hoek–Harwich (6.5–9.5 hours, *www.stenaline.co.uk*); Dieppe–Newhaven (4 hours, *www.dfdsseaways. com*); Roscoff–Plymouth (5.5 hours), Cherbourg–Poole (4.25 hours), St Malo/Cherbourg/Caen–Portsmouth (3–11 hours, *www.brittanyferries.com)*. Tickets cost more, the closer the departure time.

Booking tickets at the port is generally the most expensive.

✈ Practical airports for visiting the south-west are Exeter and Newquay. Flybe offers direct flights from London to both airports, which are reached in a good hour. There are also direct flights from Dublin to Exeter and Newquay and from Edinburgh to Exeter. US travellers who want to start at JFK will have a stopover in London if they head for Newquay or in Manchester to fly to Exeter airport. Considering the prices, we would recommend to book a flight to Newquay if you start in Toronto or Sydney.
From Bristol, you can travel relatively quickly to Devon and Cornwall. From London (ideally from Heathrow) coach and train services depart for the southwest – or you can hire a car (journey time at least 4 hours).

## BANKS

Banks *(open Mon–Fri 10am–5pm, and in some larger cities also on Sat)* and cash machines (ATMs) are located even in smaller towns, often in grocery stores, petrol stations or the pub.

## CAR HIRE

The major international car hire firms are in Exeter and Plymouth (some are out of town). The prices are competitive, but it is also advisable to book early to get a better price.

## CONSULATES AND EMBASSIES

**EMBASSY OF IRELAND**
*17 Grosvenor Place| Belgravia | London | www.dfa.ie/irish-embassy/great-britain | tel. 020 7235 2171*

**HIGH COMMISSION OF AUSTRALIA**
*Strand | London | www.uk.embassy.gov. au | tel. 020 7379 4334*

**HIGH COMMISSION OF CANADA**
*Canada House | Trafalgar Square | London | www.canadainternational.gc.ca/ united_kingdom-royaume_uni/index. aspx?lang=eng | tel. 020 7004 6000*

**U.S. EMBASSY**
*24 Grosvenor Square | London | uk.usembassy.gov | tel. 020 7499 9000*

## CUSTOMS

Within the EU the following customs guidelines apply: goods for personal use (including 800 cigarettes, 110 l beer, 60 l sparkling wine) are duty-free on entry and departure from Great Britain. There are different allowances for arrivals from outside the EU, for information check: *www.gov.uk/browse/abroad/ travel-abroad*

## DRIVING

In England you drive on the left. There are plenty of traffic lights, "give way" signs (or a thick white line in the centre of the road) and more roundabouts, even on main roads. You should give way to traffic already on the roundabout.
The maximum speed in built-up areas is generally 30 mph/48 km/h, except on single carriage country roads 60 mph (96 km/h), and on dual carriageways and motorways it is 70 mph/112 km/h. There are heavy penalties for speeding. Vehicle licence plates are now scanned to check for speeding over longer distances. The blood alcohol limit is 0.5, and it is mandatory to wear a seatbelt for all passengers. Use of a mobile phone is also banned when driving. Police are cracking down on traffic offenders – fines can be levied up to several thousand pounds. Private vehicles are also banned from driving in bus lanes.

## ELECTRICITY

The voltage is 240V and a three-pin plug is used.

## EMERGENCY SERVICES

Dial *999* or *112* as used by the European Union.

## ENTRANCE FEES

If you would like to visit the many historic sights, you can buy a weekly or annual pass for one of the major heritage organisations. *English Heritage (annual membership £54 | www.english-*

heritage.org.uk) and the *National Trust
(annual membership* £64.80 | *www.na-
tional trust.org.uk)* manage hundreds
of country houses, palaces, several pubs
and entire villages. *VisitBritain* also has
special 9 day and 16 day passes, which
you must book well in advance *(from £31
and £37)* | *www.visitbritainshop.com).*

## CURRENCY CONVERTER

| US$ | GBP | GBP | US$ |
| --- | --- | --- | --- |
| 1 | 0.75 | 10 | 13.30 |
| 2 | 1.50 | 20 | 26.60 |
| 3 | 2.25 | 25 | 33.25 |
| 4 | 3.00 | 30 | 39.90 |
| 5 | 3.75 | 40 | 53.20 |
| 6 | 4.50 | 50 | 66.50 |
| 7 | 5.25 | 70 | 93.10 |
| 8 | 6.00 | 80 | 106.40 |
| 9 | 6.75 | 95 | 126.35 |

For current exchange rates see www.xe.com

### HEALTH

The National Health Service (NHS) treats
UK and EU nationals. In case of compli-
cated accidents or return transport to
your home country, it is advisable to ar-
range travel health insurance. Pharma-
cies are found in some large supermarkets and the national pharmacy chain
Boots.

### IMMIGRATION

For citizens of most EU countries, including Ireland, an ID card is sufficient. US
citizens as well as citizens from the com-
monwealth need a valid passport; there
is no requirement for a visa for stays up
to 6 months. If you are coming by car
from abroad, you will need your driver's
license, your vehicle registration docu-
ments and the "Green Card", the international insurance card.

### INFORMATION

**VISITBRITAIN**
*www.visitbritain.com*
Information about Devon and Cornwall:
*www.visitcornwall.com / www.visitdevon.
co.uk*

### INTERNET & WIFI

Almost every hotel, restaurant and café
now offers WiFi for guests mostly free
of charge. *The Cloud* is another provider with wide WiFi coverage that is free
of charge. Register as a guest with your
smartphone which automatically logs
into this network. The cancellation of
roaming charges within the EU means
that you can also access the same data
volumes in England without incurring
additional fees. However, it is best to
check beforehand with your service
provider!

### LOCAL TIME

Greenwich Mean Time (GMT) is the
local time.

### MONEY & CREDIT CARDS

The British pound or sterling (GBP, £)
is the currency – you will not get far
in England with dollars. There are 100
pence in a pound. Great Britain has a
series of different bank notes which all
look different.
Bank notes from Scotland and Northern
Ireland can theoretically also be used in
England, although in practice this often
causes problems especially in rural areas. Credit cards are widely accepted,

even for small amounts. Contactless payment is popular with the relevant debit or credit cards as well as providers such as *ApplePay*.

Bureau de Change offices are good places to change money especially in *Marks & Spencer* department stores where you save commission fees.

## OPENING HOURS

The main opening hours are Mon–Sat 10am–5.30pm, but many grocery stores are also open before and afterwards. In major cities, there is usually a 24-hour supermarket. Retail outlets are often open until 7pm and 8pm. On Sundays, you can also go shopping in many places in Devon and Cornwall *(usually midday–5pm)*.

## PETS

Devon and Cornwall are animal friendly. Dogs are permitted to travel to Great Britain from a different EU country if they have a microchip and domestic pet passport and have been vaccinated against rabies. They must also visit a vet one to five days before travel for worming treatment. Ferries make a small extra charge for dogs that must remain in the car during the crossing.

## PHONE & MOBILE PHONE

Apart from some very rural and coastal areas and small islands, mobile phone reception in Devon and Cornwall is good. The major mobile phone providers are Vodafone, EE, Three and O2. All provid-

# WEATHER IN PLYMOUTH

| | Jan | Feb | March | April | May | June | July | Aug | Sept | Oct | Nov | Dec |
|---|---|---|---|---|---|---|---|---|---|---|---|---|
| Daytime temperatures in °C/°F | 4/39 | 4/39 | 5/41 | 6/43 | 8/46 | 11/52 | 13/55 | 13/55 | 12/54 | 9/48 | 7/45 | 5/41 |
| Night-time temperatures in °C/°F | 4/39 | 4/39 | 5/41 | 6/43 | 8/46 | 11/52 | 13/55 | 13/55 | 12/54 | 9/48 | 7/45 | 5/41 |
| ☀ | 2 | 3 | 4 | 7 | 8 | 7 | 7 | 6 | 5 | 4 | 2 | 2 |
| ☔ | 19 | 15 | 14 | 12 | 12 | 12 | 14 | 14 | 15 | 16 | 17 | 18 |
| 〰 | 9/48 | 9/48 | 9/48 | 9/48 | 11/52 | 13/55 | 15/59 | 16/61 | 15/59 | 14/57 | 12/54 | 11/52 |

ers also offer pre-paid cards. Reasonable tariffs for these cards are offered by Virgin, Tesco, Sainsbury's and Three. The country code for England is 0044. When calling from abroad, omit the '0' of the area code or the first zero on mobile numbers. The UK dial code for the USA and Canada is 001, for Australia 0061, and for Ireland 00353. Omit any leading '1' in North American numbers and any first zero in Australian or Irish numbers.

## POST

Post offices in rural areas and increasingly in larger cities are now found in stationery shops, petrol stations or supermarkets, and opening hours are the same. Official post offices are open from Mon–Fri 9am–5.30pm and Sat 9am– 12.30pm. To send letters and postcards to Europe, you need to buy a stamp for £1.17.

## TAXIS

Taxi fares are as expensive as in European countries. It is best to phone for a cab (numbers vary depending on location). Taxi ranks outside London are rare.

## TIPPING

In restaurants, depending on how happy you are with the service, it is usual to add about 10 per cent to the bill – unless a service charge is already shown. This can be the case in touristy areas but it is not universal. Hotel staff and taxi drivers will be happy to receive a small tip.

# ROAD ATLAS

The green line indicates the Discovery Tour "Devon & Cornwall at a glance"
The blue line indicates the other Discovery Tours

All tours are also marked on the pull-out map

Photo: Exmoor

# Exploring Devon and Cornwall

The map on the back cover shows how the area has been sub-divided

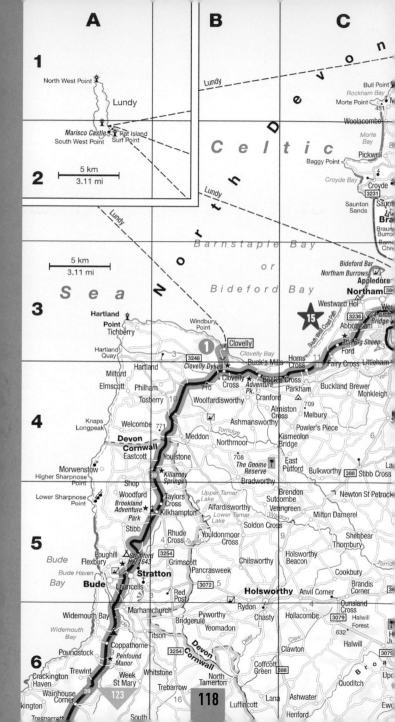

## A

**1**

North West Point �ᵢ

Lundy

Marisco Castle ⛨ Rat Island
South West Point ⛨ Surf Point

**2**

5 km
3.11 mi

5 km
3.11 mi

*Sea*

**3**

Hartland ⛨
**Point**
Tichberry

Hartland
Quay

Milford
Elmscott   Philham

Knaps    Tosberry
Longpeak

Welcombe

**4**

**Devon**
**Cornwall**
Eastcott    Youlstone

Morwenstow ♦
Higher Sharpnose
Point

Lower Sharpnose    Shop
Point
Woodford
*Brookland*
*Adventure*    Taylors
*Park*    Cross
Kilkhampton

Stibb

Poughill    Rhude
**5**    Flexbury    4 Cross
*Bude Haven*
Bay    **Bude**
Launcells

Widemouth Bay

*Widemouth*    Itson
*Bay*

Poundstock    Coppathorne
**6**    *Penfound*
Trewint    *Manor*
Crackington    Week
Haven    St Mary    Whitstone
Wainhouse    39    **123**
kington    Corner
Tresparrett    South

## B

Lundy

Lundy

Lundy

Windbury
Point

3248    Clovelly
⭐ Dykes    Clovelly Bay
3    Buck's Mills
Clovelly    Horns
710   Cross    Cross
Adventure    Buck's
Pk ⭐    Cross
Woolfardisworthy    Parkham
Cranford

Torridge    Ashmansworthy

771    Meddon    Northmoor
708    East
*The Gnome*    Putford
*Reserve*
Bradworthy

*Upper Tamar*
*Lake*    Brendon
Alfardisworthy    Sutcombe
Killarney ⭐    *Lower Tamar*    Venngreen
*Springs*    *Lake*
Youldonmoor    Soldon Cross
Cross

Grimscott    Chilsworthy
Stamford    3254
HW 1643
**Stratton**    Pancrasweek
3    3072
Marhamchurch    Red    5
Post
Pyworthy
Bridgerule    Yeomadon    Chasty    Rydon

**Devon**    North    Clawton
*Cornwall*    Tamerton
16    **118**    Trebarrow    Lana
Luffincott    Henford

## C

*Devon*

Bull Point
*Rockham Bay*
Morte Point
451
Woolacombe

*Celtic*    *Morte*
*Bay*

Baggy Point    Pickwell

*Croyde Bay*
Croyde
3231
Saunton    Saun
Sands
**Bra**
Braun
Burro
Barn
Chi

*Barnstaple Bay*
*or*
*Bideford Bar*    ♦
*Northam Burrows* ♦    Appledore
*Bideford Bay*    **Northam** 38
Westward Ho! ♦
⭐**15**    South West Coast Path    Wes
3236
Abbotsham
*The Big Sheep*    Bridge
Ford    39    Littleham
Fairy Cross
11
Buckland Brewer    Monkleigh

709
Almiston    Melbury
Cross
Kismeolon
Bridge
6

Newton St Petrock

Milton Damerel
9
Shebbear
Thornbury
Holsworthy
Beacon    Cookbury
Brandis
Corner
**Holsworthy**    Anvil Corner
3
Ounsland
Cross
Hollacombe    3079    Halwill
Forest
632    Halwill    3075
Coffcott
Green    Claw    Ashwater
388    Quoditch
Broa
Up
Ashwater
Henford    Ewc

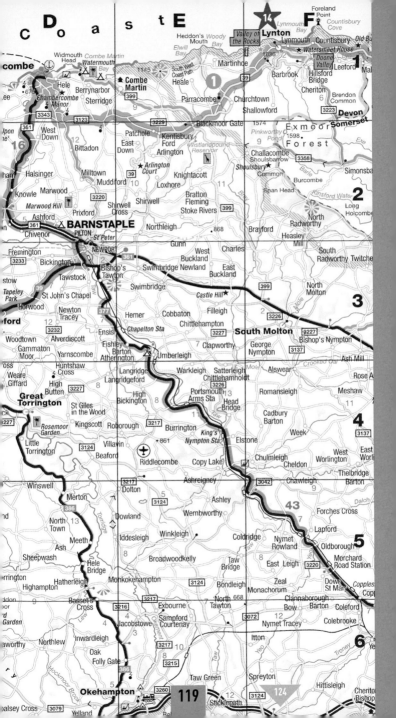

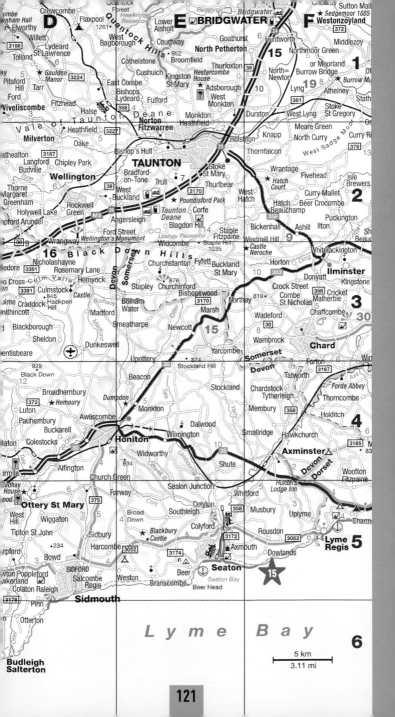

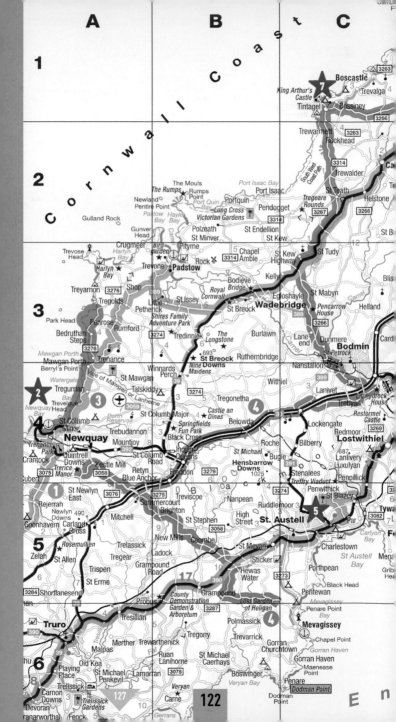

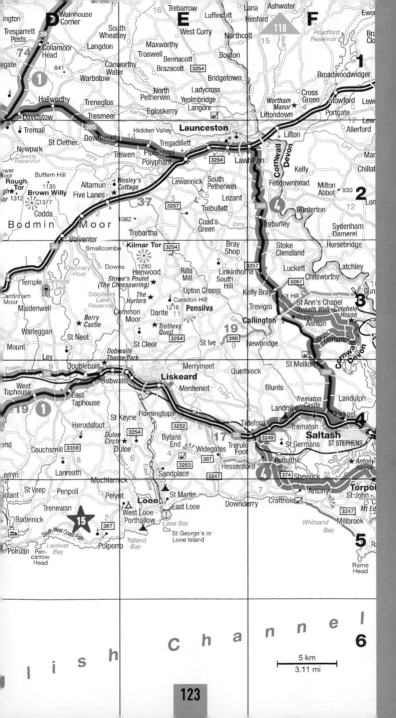

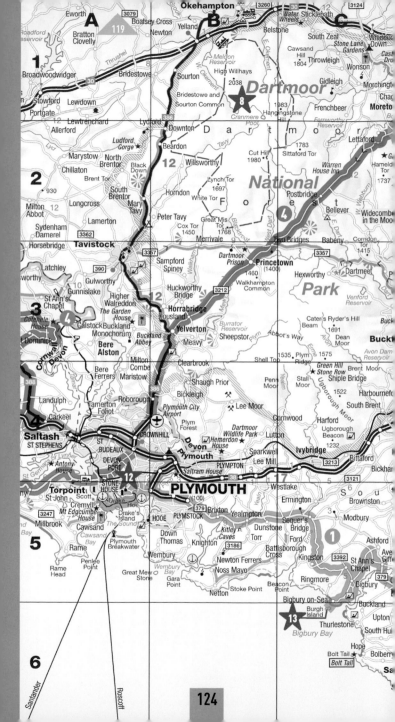

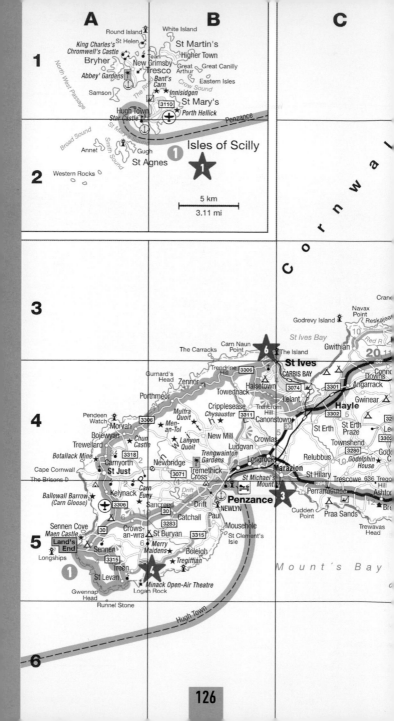

## A

**1**

Round Island 🕯
St Helen ⛪
White Island
King Charles's
Chromwell's Castle ⛪
Bryher
Tean
New Grimsby
Tresco
Abbey' Gardens ⛪
Samson

St Martin's
Higher Town
Great
Arthur
Great Canilly
Eastern Isles

*North West Passage*
*The Po*
Bant's
Carn
Innisidgen
St Mary's
Hugh Town
Star Castle ⛪
3110
Porth Hellick
*Crow Sound*

Penzance

## B

**2**

*Broad Sound*
Annet
Gugh
St Agnes
Smith Sound
*St Mary's*
Western Rocks

**①  Isles of Scilly**

⭐**1**

5 km
3.11 mi

## C

*C o r n w a l l*

*C o*
*r n*
*w a*

**3**

Godrevy Island ⛫
Navax
Point Reskajea
Crane

*St Ives Bay*
The Carracks
Carn Naun
Point
⭐**6**
The Island
**St Ives**
Gwithian
10
*Red R*
**20** 11

**4**

Gurnard's
Head
Zennor
Trendrine
Hill
3306
CARBIS BAY
3074
Conno
Downs
Angarrack

Porthmeor
Towednack
Halsetown
3301
Gwinear
**Hayle**

Pendeen
Watch ⛫
Morvah
Men-
an-Tol ★
Mulfra
Quoit
Chysauster
Cripplesease
Trencrom
Hill
3311
Lelant
3302
St Erth
Praze
5
Le
32

Bojewyan
Trewellard
Chun
Castle ★
Lanyon
Quoit ★
New Mill
Canonstown
80
St Erth
Townshend
3302

Botallack Mine ★
Carnyorth
Newbridge
3071
Trengwainton
Gardens
Ludgvan
Longrock
5
Relubbus
3280
Godolphin
House ⛫

Cape Cornwall
**St Just**
Tremethick
Cross
4
**Marazion**
St Hilary
Trescowe 636 Trego
Hill
Ashto

The Brisons ᴅ
Ballowall Barrow ★
(Carn Gloose)
Kelynack
3306
Carn
Euny ★
Sancreed
30
Drift
Reser
Drift
*St Michael's
Mount* ⛫
**Penzance**
**NEWLYN**
Perranuthn
Bre

**5**

Sennen Cove
Maen Castle ★
**Land's
End**
Longships ⛫
①
30
Sennen
3315
Treen
St Levan
Gwennap
Head
Runnel Stone

Crows-
an-wra
3306
Catchall
3283
Paul
Mousehole
Cudden
Point
St Clement's
Isle
Praa Sands
Trewavas
Head

St Buryan
3315
Merry
Maidens ★
Boleigh
Tregiffian ★
⭐
Minack Open-Air Theatre
Logan Rock

*M o u n t ′ s   B a y*

**6**

Hugh Town

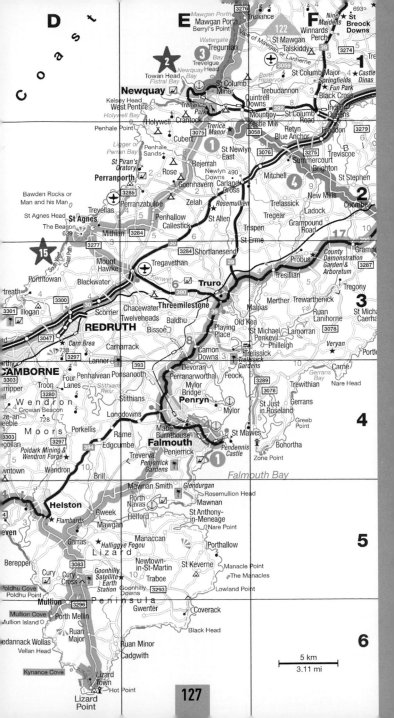

# KEY TO ROAD ATLAS

|  | |  |
|---|---|---|
| Autobahn mit Anschlussstelle und Anschlussnummern | Viernheim 45 49 36 24 12 | Motorway with junction and junction number |
| Autobahn in Bau mit voraussichtlichem Fertigstellungsdatum | Datum   Date | Motorway under construction with expected date of opening |
| Rasthaus mit Übernachtung · Raststätte | Kassel  X | Hotel, motel · Restaurant |
| Kiosk · Tankstelle | | Snackbar · Filling-station |
| Autohof · Parkplatz mit WC | P | Truckstop · Parking place with WC |
| Autobahn-Gebührenstelle | | Toll station |
| Autobahnähnliche Schnellstraße | | Dual carriageway with motorway characteristics |
| Fernverkehrsstraße | | Trunk road |
| Verbindungsstraße | | Main road |
| Nebenstraßen | | Secondary roads |
| Fahrweg · Fußweg | | Carriageway · Footpath |
| Gebührenpflichtige Straße | | Toll road |
| Straße für Kraftfahrzeuge gesperrt | X X X X X | Road closed for motor vehicles |
| Straße für Wohnanhänger gesperrt | | Road closed for caravans |
| Straße für Wohnanhänger nicht empfehlenswert | | Road not recommended for caravans |
| Autofähre · Autozug-Terminal | | Car ferry · Autorail station |
| Hauptbahn · Bahnhof · Tunnel | | Main line railway · Station · Tunnel |
| Besonders sehenswertes kulturelles Objekt | ♪ Neuschwanstein | Cultural site of particular interest |
| Besonders sehenswertes landschaftliches Objekt | ✱ Breitachklamm | Landscape of particular interest |
| MARCO POLO Erlebnistour 1 | | MARCO POLO Discovery Tour 1 |
| MARCO POLO Erlebnistouren | | MARCO POLO Discovery Tours |
| MARCO POLO Highlight | ★ | MARCO POLO Highlight |
| Landschaftlich schöne Strecke | | Route with beautiful scenery |
| Touristenstraße | Hanse-Route | Tourist route |
| Museumseisenbahn | | Tourist train |
| Kirche, Kapelle · Kirchenruine Kloster · Klosterruine | ♪ ♪ ♪ ♪ | Church, chapel · Church ruin Monastery · Monastery ruin |
| Schloss, Burg · Burgruine Turm · Radio-, Fernsehturm | ♪ ♪ ♪ ♪ | Palace, castle · Castle ruin Tower · Radio or TV tower |
| Leuchtturm · Windmühle Denkmal · Soldatenfriedhof | ♪ ✗ ♪ ⊞ | Lighthouse · Windmill Monument · Military cemetery |
| Ruine, frühgeschichtliche Stätte · Höhle Hotel, Gasthaus, Berghütte · Heilbad | ∴ ∩ ♠ ♨ | Archaeological excavation, ruins · Cave Hotel, inn, refuge · Spa |
| Campingplatz · Jugendherberge Schwimmbad, Erlebnisbad, Strandbad · Golfplatz | ⚊ ⚊ △ ⚊ ⚊ | Camping site · Youth hostel Swimming pool, leisure pool, beach · Golf-course |
| Botanischer Garten, sehenswerter Park · Zoologischer Garten | | Botanical gardens, interesting park · Zoological garden |
| Bedeutendes Bauwerk · Bedeutendes Areal | ▪ ◻ | Important building · Important area |
| Verkehrsflughafen · Regionalflughafen | ✈ ⊕ | Airport · Regional airport |
| Flugplatz · Segelflugplatz | ⊕ ⊶ | Airfield · Gliding site |
| Boots- und Jachthafen | ⚓ | Marina |

# FOR YOUR NEXT TRIP...

# MARCO POLO TRAVEL GUIDES

**A**lgarve
Amsterdam
Andalucia
Athens
Australia
Austria
**B**ali & Lombok
Bangkok
Barcelona
Berlin
Brazil
Bruges
Brussels
Budapest
Bulgaria
**C**alifornia
Cambodia
Canada East
Canada West / Rockies
& Vancouver
Cape Town &
Garden Route
Cape Verde
Channel Islands
Chicago & The Lakes
China
Cologne
Copenhagen
Corfu
Costa Blanca
& Valencia
Costa Brava
Costa del Sol & Granada
Crete
Cuba
Cyprus (North and
South)
**D**evon & Cornwall
Dresden
Dubai

Dublin
Dubrovnik &
Dalmatian Coast
**E**dinburgh
Egypt
Egypt Red Sea Resorts
**F**inland
Florence
Florida
French Atlantic Coast
French Riviera
(Nice, Cannes & Monaco)
Fuerteventura
**G**ran Canaria
Greece
**H**amburg
Hong Kong & Macau
**I**celand
India
India South
Ireland
Israel
Istanbul
Italy
**J**apan
Jordan
**K**os
Krakow
**L**ake Garda
Lanzarote
Las Vegas
Lisbon
London
Los Angeles
**M**adeira & Porto Santo
Madrid
Mallorca
Malta & Gozo
Mauritius
Menorca

Milan
Montenegro
Morocco
Munich
**N**aples & Amalfi Coast
New York
New Zealand
Norway
**O**slo
Oxford
**P**aris
Peru & Bolivia
Phuket
Portugal
Prague
**R**hodes
Rome
**S**alzburg
San Francisco
Santorini
Sardinia
Scotland
Seychelles
Shanghai
Sicily
Singapore
South Africa
Sri Lanka
Stockholm
Switzerland
**T**enerife
Thailand
Turkey
Turkey South Coast
Tuscany
**U**nited Arab Emirates
USA Southwest
(Las Vegas, Colorado,
New Mexico, Arizona
& Utah)
**V**enice
Vienna
Vietnam
**Z**akynthos & Ithaca,
Kefalonia, Lefkas

The travel guides with
**Insider Tips**

# INDEX

All sights and destinations mentioned in this guide are listed in this index. Page numbers in bold refer to the main entry.

# CREDITS

# WRITE TO US

e-mail: info@marcopologuides.co.uk
Did you have a great holiday?
Is there something on your mind?
Whatever it is, let us know!
Whether you want to praise, alert us to errors or give us a personal tip – MARCO POLO would be pleased to hear from you.
We do everything we can to provide the very latest information for your trip.

Nevertheless, despite all of our authors' thorough research, errors can creep in. MARCO POLO does not accept any liability for this. Please contact us by e-mail or post.
MARCO POLO Travel Publishing Ltd
Pinewood, Chineham Business Park
Crockford Lane, Chineham
Basingstoke, Hampshire RG24 8AL
United Kingdom

**PICTURE CREDITS**
Cover Photograph: Bodmin Moor, Wheal Jenkin Mine (Laif/Loop Images: C. Joiner)
Photos: AWL Images: P. Adams (45, 115); Getty Images: N. Bidgood (4 top, 26/27), W. Gray (19 top), pjohnson1 (18 bottom), J. Taylor (106), A. Tomlinson (107); Getty Images/Caiaimage: P. Bradbury (29); Getty Images/Westend61 (3); huber-images: J. Banks (74), P. Canali (12/13, 17, 32/33, 48/49, 86/87, 95), J. Foulkes (2, 5, 38, 66, 73, 108 top), M. Rellini (54, 70, 101), S. Wasek (57, 82); Interfoto/FLPA: A. Wheatley (120/121); Interfoto/National Trust Picture Library: C. Lacey (69); Laif: E. Häberle (19 bottom); Laif/Allpix: I. Jones (20/21); Laif/Le Figaro Magazine: Rogery (65); Laif/Loop Images: C. Button (4 bottom, 60/61), M. Gibson (42), C. Joiner (1 top, 76/77, 78), P. Prince (flap right), A. Ray (62), G. Scammell (106/107), S. Staszczuk (14/15, 109); Laif/robertharding: A. Burton (25), A. Copson (10), M. Nolan (9), E. Rooney (37); Look/age fotostock (8, 41, 58, 108 bottom); Look/robertharding (50); mauritius images: maskot (18 centre), S. Vidler (31), J. Warburton-Lee/W. Gray (30/31); mauritius images/Alamy: K. Birtland (53), S. Burt (6), I. Dagnall (47), geogphotos (7), C. Mannings (85), S. Maycock (11), D. Pattison (81), E. Westmacott (105); mauritius images/Bluegreen Pictures: M. Thomas (flap left); mauritius images/Cultura (98/99, 102/103); mauritius images/Foodanddrinkphotos (28 right, 30); mauritius images/Image Source: B. Stevens (28 left); mauritius images/imagebroker: S. Gabriel (91), A. Nekrasov (18 top); mauritius images/nature picture library/2020VISION: A. Mustard (34); Visum/Panos Pictures: A. Testa (22)

**1st edition 2018**
Worldwide Distribution: Marco Polo Travel Publishing Ltd, Pinewood, Chineham Business Park, Crockford Lane, Basingstoke, Hampshire RG24 8AL, United Kingdom. Email: sales@marcopolouk.com
© MAIRDUMONT GmbH & Co. KG, Ostfildern
Chief editor: Marion Zorn
Author: Michael Pohl; editor: Corinna Walkenhorst
Programme supervision: Lucas Forst-Gill, Susanne Heimburger, Johanna Jiranek, Nikolai Michaelis, Kristin Wittemann, Tim Wohlbold; picture editor: Anja Schlatterer
Cartography road atlas and pull-out map: © MAIRDUMONT, Ostfildern
Cover design, p. 1, pull-out map cover: Karl Anders – Büro für Visual Stories, Hamburg; design inside: milchhof:atelier, Berlin; design p. 2/3, Discovery Tours: Susan Chaaban Dipl.-Des. (FH)
Translated from German by Suzanne Kirkbright
Editorial office: SAW Communications, Redaktionsbüro Dr. Sabine A. Werner, Mainz: Julia Gilcher, Cosima Talhouni, Dr. Sabine A. Werner; prepress: SAW Communications, Mainz, in cooperation with alles mit Medien, Mainz

# DOS & DON'TS 👆

**A few things to bear in mind when travelling in Devon and Cornwall**

## DO SHOP LOCALLY

If you see a "Farm Shop" sign on your travels, do try to make a stop. By supporting local businesses and shopping locally you will be rewarded with the best and freshest produce the area has to offer.

## DON'T TRAVEL ON PUBLIC HOLIDAYS

Devon and Cornwall are incredibly popular – even with the locals. Every bank holiday the roads heading for the south-west are packed like at the start of the school holidays (mid-July to early September). You should try to avoid travelling at these times and enjoy more of your stay.

## DO TRY THE SEAFOOD

From crab shacks to oyster bars – some of the best seafood in the world can be found in this region. Go for the catch of the day and you'll be in for a culinary treat!

## DON'T OVERPLAN

As tempting as it can be to cram your itinerary full of stops, life in Devon and Cornwall moves at a slower pace. Do as the locals do and take time to relax and enjoy each destination you visit.

## DO BOOK IN ADVANCE

Especially in the summer months, Devon and Cornwall become very busy with holidaymakers. To avoid disappointment, be sure to book your accommodation well in advance. This also goes for restaurants, especially at weekends.

## DON'T UNDERESTIMATE THE WEATHER

Coastal hiking paths are wonderful, but you should avoid walking during stormy weather. You may not have a chance to turn back for miles. If you get caught in a thunderstorm here, it can be life threatening.

## DO EAT A CORNISH PASTY

Nowadays Cornwall's national dish comes filled with all manner of meaty and delicious fillings and is a satisfying snack best enjoyed by the seaside.